CW00967716

THE DRUG OFFICER'S COMPANION

Paul Harper
Steve Dalrymple

Further titles available from Police Review Publishing Co:
● **Action Stations: A Guide to OSPRE Part II** ● **Beat Officer's Companion**
● **Scottish Beat Officer's Companion** ● **Traffic Officer's Companion**
● **Custody Officer's Companion** ● **Financial Investigator's Companion**
● **PACE – a Guide for the Practitioner** ● **Points to Prove**
● **Summonses and Charges** ● **Taking Statements** ● **Child Protection Manual**
● **Street Survival Skills** ● **Practical Police Management**
● **Special Constable's Manual**
To order or for further details phone 01708 381204 or fax 01708 381211

No part of this publication may be reproduced
or transmitted in any form or by any means, or
stored in any retrieval system of any nature, without prior
written permission, except for permitted fair dealing under
the Copyright, Designs and Patents Act 1988, or in accordance
with the terms of a licence issued by the Copyright Licensing Agency
in respect of photocopying and/or reprographic reproduction.
Application for permission for other use of copyright material
including permission to reproduce extracts in other published works
shall be made to the publishers. Full acknowledgement of
author, publisher and source must be given.

© Paul Harper
Steve Dalrymple   1997

ISBN 085164 077X

**Police Review
Publishing Co**

**Celcon House
289-293, High Holborn
London WC1V 7HU**

Illustrations by Rich King
Proof read and indexed by Mandy Preece, Bitterne Village, Southampton
Printed and bound in Great Britain by
The Greenacre Press, Northfleet, Kent

THE AUTHORS

Paul Harper has experience as a custody officer and has been heavily involved in teaching and writing about PACE in various contexts, including interviewing. He has been responsible for preparing custody officers for the rigours of that role while being a trainer at a regional training centre. As a shift inspector at a busy division in Kingston Upon Hull, he regularly authorises searches of drug suspects' homes and oversees street level investigations.

Steve Dalrymple is an experienced drug squad officer, having served as a detective constable and detective sergeant, both before and after the introduction of PACE. Like Paul he is a former trainer who has lectured on interviewing, drugs and PACE, to a wide range of audiences both inside and outside the police service. As an inspector with Humberside Police, he now sees the rewards of the training he has given to colleagues.

ACKNOWLEDGEMENTS

The authors would like to thank the many people from various organisations such as health, education, drugs advisory and rehabilitation units, together with the forensic science service and the Home Office who have all assisted with this project. Without exception they have willingly given valuable time to contribute to the accuracy of the book.

Particular thanks are due to the following for their efforts and advice:

Sue Mitchell
Sara Bishop
Barbara Jenkyn
Ian Oxley
John Pilkington.

FOREWORD

In the short time it takes to read this foreword, a number of crimes will have been committed to finance a drugs habit. Some abusers, possibly first time users, will suffer illness from overdosing or injecting and may even die as a result. The victims of these tragedies suffer heavily, as do the parents, friends and relatives of those who abuse drugs.

Police officers throughout the country are working tirelessly to combat the pernicious effects of drug misuse and their determination to fight drug-related crime is matched by similar efforts from health workers, teachers, carers and counsellors who have a vital role to play in education, prevention and rehabilitation. By working together with a common objective of breaking into the drugs/crime circle and, by so doing, reducing the number of victims, we have a real chance of making a difference.

All police officers have a responsibility to investigate offences relating to the Misuse of Drugs at street and community level and that includes the investigation of criminal offences linked to drug abuse – to feed a habit, possession of drugs and local dealing.

Humberside Police recognises the need to assist officers to carry out that responsibility safely and effectively through an increased awareness about drugs.

This book is a development of that recognition to support the needs of street level officers and their supervisors.

Remember that a successful enforcement and diversion strategy can ease other burdens on the service by reducing crime and significantly improving the quality of life for members of the public.

D A Leonard QPM BSc [ECON]
Chief Constable
Humberside Police

Contents

Chapter 1

INTRODUCTION

Drug abuse is a disease from which no country and no section of modern society seems immune. It brings ruthless hardened criminals and weak and vulnerable users together in a combination which is potentially lethal. All the indicators, seizures, arrests, research and social surveys, confirm that drug abuse is on the increase. More and more young people are experimenting with so-called soft drugs, putting themselves and our future at risk. Co-operation between governments, law enforcement agencies, professionals, schools and families is essential if we are to win the fight against drugs.

As the thin blue line becomes ever more stretched in the fight against drugs, police chiefs are having to deploy resources more effectively, with regional drugs wings and crime squads being directed at regional, national and international targets, and force and county drugs squads concentrating on drugs dealers. That leaves the street level for local officers to police, adding drugs to their already heavy workload. This book is aimed at street level officers and their supervisors, providing a quick and easy reference and the background knowledge vital for successful drugs investigations. In many ways it makes good sense to include drugs within the range of policing tasks undertaken by the local copper, in as much as many crimes result directly from drug dependence. The drug abusers, themselves victims, create a vicious circle of escalating crime. Often they become suppliers in order to maintain their own habit, with drugs offences and general crime clustering around the dealers, widening the circle of crime.

The only way to break the circle is by returning to two of our primary functions, the detection and prevention of crime, by working with Customs and Excise officers, forensic scientists and the public to detect drug offences.

We must work with teachers, health and social services, youth workers, probation officers and voluntary agencies, to educate, rehabilitate and support drug users to help them kick the habit and prevent further drug and general offending. Law enforcement alone is not the answer and attempting to involve the abuser with one of the many caring organisations is a pro-active step in breaking the drugs-crime circle, saving others from becoming victims of drugs or victims of crime.

That is not to say that we should neglect our other primary duty – to prosecute offenders – and the following chapters will ensure that you collect, package, protect and introduce evidence properly, thus safeguarding yourself and your career in the process of prosecution.

Think of the book as a filing cabinet stuffed with relevant information, with each chapter acting as a drawer containing a series of files dedicated to one aspect of dealing with drugs.

▶ Chapter One is an Introduction

▶ Chapter Two explores the drugs scene and lists the commonly abused substances from Cocaine to Magic Mushrooms, including some 'not controlled' such as solvents. The chapter describes how they are abused, their effects and the dangers they present, as well as providing relevant information about their classes, street names, clinical titles (used in framing charges), and signs and symptoms of abuse, etc. The chapter ends by reproducing the key schedule of 'controlled' drugs.

▶ Chapter Three provides information intended to protect you during contact with drugs abusers and gives vital first aid advice to help you on the street. It covers areas such as protecting yourself from HIV, AIDS, Hepatitis and other risks and provides clear, simple emergency procedures specific to drugs-related illness.

▶ Chapter Four covers your powers of search and seizure and incorporates legislation, Codes of Practice and decided cases to help you negotiate the minefield of legislation dealing with searching people, vehicles and vessels

▶ Chapter Five extends the explanation of powers of search and seizure to premises. It covers search with consent, with and without warrant, the conduct of a search as determined by the Codes of Practice, seizing evidence, action to be taken after searches, together with practical tips concerning how to plan, brief, prepare and carry out searches and advice about children and informants.

▶ Chapter Six is concerned exclusively with gathering and safeguarding evidence. It includes the initial recovery of drugs, protecting evidence, packaging, exhibiting and documenting drugs, dealing with cannabis, continuity of evidence, and presumptive testing. This is combined with the standard and the improvised methods to achieve best practice no matter what the prevailing conditions.

▶ Chapter Seven is centred upon the drugs interview itself. It takes you through all the stages of planning, preparation, introducing exhibits, unsolicited comments, significant statements and special warnings, and gives practical tips on interview techniques. It also contains specific advice in relation to drugs trafficking and informants, and includes a full list of the points to prove for all main drug offences, supported by relevant decided cases and examples plus a glossary of drugs terms to enhance your performance in interview.

S

Authors' note for officers serving in Scotland

Scotland retains its own unique legal system, the development of which has been influenced by both Franco-Germanic law and English law. Consequently Scots law is quite different from English law

One effect of having this hybrid legal system is that the Scots courts regard the laws pertaining to England, Wales and Northern Ireland as 'foreign laws', and are not automatically bound by the precedent decisions of other UK courts, even where the precedent relates to legislation operating in Scotland, eg the Misuse of Drugs Act 1971.

However, a Scots court may be persuaded to accept a precedent set by a court in another part of the UK, and apply the decision to the case it is dealing with, provided the 'foreign precedent' does not conflict with the fundamental principles of Scots law.

To assist Scottish officers, John Pilkington, a former inspector with Strathclyde Police who produces the Police (Scotland) Promotion Exams series in *Police Review*, has kindly prepared the footnotes which accompany this book to direct attention to the equivalent areas of Scottish legislation relevant to drugs investigations. All these footnotes are presented as here, boxed, with the symbol 'S' in the margin.

Chapter 2

THE DRUGS SCENE

INTRODUCTION

With the possible exception of illicit sex, there is no greater social taboo than that of illicit drug taking. Those who indulge in 'recreational drug taking' are seen as somehow separate from society, being part of an alien culture. This chapter aims to give an insight into the 'drug scene', focusing particularly upon those substances which are commonly abused and which are subject to control by the Misuse of Drugs Act 1971.

There are hundreds of drugs available in Britain, of which only a small minority are routinely abused. Certain drugs are designated as 'controlled drugs' under the Act and are divided into three categories or classes, based upon their harmful effects – ranging from Class A which is the most harmful, to Class C, which is the least harmful.

In this chapter we will describe the substances most frequently encountered by those who work in and around the drugs scene, taking each substance in turn. We will look at how the drug is abused; what its effects are; what dangers it presents, as well as providing relevant information about its place in the drugs scene. These descriptions include street names, common names and clinical titles used in framing charges, as well as giving advice on what to look out for in terms of signs, symptoms and behaviour.

The chapter concludes by listing the substances contained in Schedule 2 of the Misuse of Drugs Act 1971 together with an explanation of the Misuse of Drugs Regulations 1985.

THE SUBSTANCES DESCRIBED INCLUDE:

[A] Classes of Drugs

[1] CLASS A

1.i Cocaine *[Common name]*

Coke, Snow, 'C', Charlie *[Street names]*

Crack *[See note overleaf]*

Cocaine *[Proper name – used for wording a charge]*

Q. What is cocaine?
A. Cocaine is a shiny white powder, some say 'lustrous'. It is derived from the Andean Coca Shrub and is a powerful stimulant.

Q. How is it abused?
A. Cocaine can be, and often is, injected, sometimes mixed with heroin to form a cocktail. However it is most commonly 'sniffed' or 'snorted' up the nose, through a tube, usually a drinking straw (although the richer users have been known to use a large denomination bank note instead). It then enters the blood supply via the nasal membrane.

Q. What are its effects?
A. When injected, a 'rush' is experienced, which provides feelings of exhilaration, well-being, strength, alertness and an abundance of energy and elation. This rush soon peaks and is followed by a rapid return to earth, known as 'coming down'. Continued use may cause hallucinations and paranoia. It is addictive.

Q. What danger does it present to me?

A. When dealing with those who inject, the searching and recovery of related 'items' can present the risk of a 'needle stick' injury and hence HIV, hepatitis, etc.

Q. What else do I need to know?

A. Cocaine in various forms has become an extremely popular drug of abuse, especially in the inner cities. It occasionally comes in small paper 'wraps', often cut from the shiny paper of catalogues and magazines. Small mirrors and razor blades are sometimes used to prepare the substance for use or packaging.

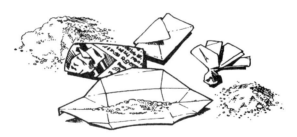

Note: Crack Cocaine

Crack cocaine is also becoming widely available. It is essentially cocaine which has been treated with chemicals to allow it to be 'smoked'. It comes in the form of small rocks about a quarter inch in size, varying in colour between white and dark cream. It is often carried in a small phial or bottle about one inch in height containing three or four 'rocks'.

See note regarding the monitoring of seizures of crack cocaine in chapter 6.

1.ii Ecstasy (XTC) *[Common name]*

'E', Brown Biscuits, Disco Burgers *[Street names]*

Methylenedioxymethylamphetamine
[Proper name – used for wording a charge]

Q. What is ecstasy?
A. Ecstasy is amphetamine-based and, although sometimes found as a white powder, it is commonly obtained in the form of colourless, red, or white, capsules containing a light brown powder – though light brown, yellow or pink tablets, similar in shape and size to paracetamol, are also available.

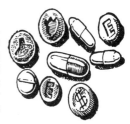

Q. How is it abused?
A. It is taken orally, usually in tablet or capsule form.

Q. What are its effects?
A. The effects begin after about 20 minutes and last for hours. On the plus side, it makes the user feel calm, friendly, and confident, yet gives endless energy and heightens perception of colour and sound. On the minus side, in prolonged or higher doses it creates anxiety, depression, fatigue, insomnia, paranoia and physical symptoms such as dehydration, stiffness and a dangerous rise in body temperature.

Q. What danger does it present to me?
A. It represents no danger to the non-user. However, be aware when dealing with users. People with heart conditions, high blood pressure, epilepsy or mental illness are at particular risk from the drug and need careful monitoring.

Q. What else do I need to know?

A. Ecstasy remains particularly popular on the 'rave' and 'club' scenes and is often sold at such events, where unscrupulous traders may sell other substances on the pretext of being Ecstasy, including LSD, Amphetamines and even dog worming tablets. Equally, club owners and organisers often sell soft drinks at wildly inflated prices, knowing that users will pay anything to quench their thirst.

Class A

1.iii Heroin *[Common name]*

Smack, Junk, 'H' *[Street names]*

Diamorphine *[Proper name – used for wording a charge]*

Q. What is Heroin?
A. Heroin is an opiate, derived from the opium poppy via the drug morphine. It is likely to be found as a fine brown powder which may smell like vinegar, though in its pure form it comes as a white powder.

Q. How is it abused?
A. It can be swallowed, dissolved in water and injected to maximise the effect, sniffed up the nose like cocaine, or smoked (this is often done by placing it on silver foil, heating with a lighter and inhaling the fumes, ie 'chasing the dragon').

Street Heroin is often 'cut' (adulterated) with other risky substances, such as scouring powder, talcum, powdered milk, even brick dust, creating added risk to the abuser.

Q. What are its effects?
A. On the plus side, it gives a feeling of warmth, well-being and drowsiness, replacing fear and tension with a feeling of euphoria and creating a feeling of detachment from reality. On the minus side it is extremely addictive, causing the user to become dependent, requiring regular or increased doses to maintain a feeling of normality. It can also produce immediate and unpleasant side effects like nausea and vomiting.

Q. What danger does it present to me?
A. Needle sharing is common among abusers of this drug, increasing the risk of HIV, hepatitis and other diseases to those using and to anyone suffering a needle stick injury.

Q. What else do I need to know?
A. Abusers of this drug are commonly known as 'smackheads' and some will go to any lengths to obtain and conceal the substance. It is often sold in paper wraps, polythene bags, or Clingfilm and is sometimes concealed in a condom, secreted in a body orifice. Items associated with heroin include silver foil, syringes and needles, mechanical or electric scales and 'burned' spoons, all of which may contain traces of heroin. One unusual item associated with heroin abuse is a 'Jiff lemon' which is squirted directly onto the heroin, contained on a spoon, to make it soluble for injecting. Cotton wool is often used as a filter to gather impurities as the solution is drawn into the syringe from the spoon.

1.iv LSD *[Common name]*
Acid, Trips *[Street names]*
Lysergide *[Proper name – used for wording a charge]*

Q. What is LSD?

A. LSD is a synthetic white powder which is impregnated onto small card squares, measuring between one quarter and half an inch. These squares often carry colourful, attractive designs featuring cartoon characters, although plain blotting paper is sometime a means of disguise. LSD has been known to be impregnated on gelatine-based substances and placed between strips of Sellotape for easy distribution. These are known as 'micro dots'.

Q. How is it abused?

A. The square, blotting paper, or micro dot containing the LSD is taken by mouth, and absorbed through the tongue or swallowed whole. It takes effect after about 20 minutes and a 'trip' may last for up to five hours depending on the strength.

Q. What are its effects?

A. The drug causes hallucinations which are unpredictable, and which are sometimes experienced as 'flashbacks', as the effects are repeated unexpectedly in the future, long after taking the drug. Some argue that the user's frame of mind acts with the drug to determine whether the user has a good or bad trip. It causes unpleasant effects such as panic attacks, dizziness or depression, and is likely to make the user psychotic, or seriously anxious.

Q. What danger does it present to me?
A. LSD can be absorbed directly through the skin, and any person handling it directly could suffer its effects.

Q. What else do I need to know?
> **A.** This is an extremely popular drug among people who attend 'raves', sometimes making them act dangerously, to the extent of causing damage or death while seeking to escape from a 'bad trip' or suffering hallucinations whilst driving.
>
> It is easily concealed, often simply kept in a wallet or purse with other pieces of paper.

Class A

1.v Methadone *[Common name]*

Meth *[Street name]*

Methadone
[Proper name – used for wording a charge]

Q. What is Methadone?

A. Methadone is a synthetic substance often prescribed for heroin addicts to wean them off the drug. It comes in three forms, in a phial for injection (usually only prescribed for illness), as a white tablet (physeptone), or as a mixture which looks like a linctus, being a thick, viscous liquid which is the most common form of the drug. The liquid is sweet smelling and similar in colour and consistency to green Fairy Liquid, hence it is sometimes hidden in Fairy Liquid bottles.

Q. How is it abused?
A. It is normally taken orally, often swigged directly from the bottle.

Q. What are its effects?
A. Its effects are similar to those of heroin *(see page 11)* without the 'rush' craved by heroin users.

Q. What danger does it present to me?
A. In itself it represents little danger, provided that you wash your hands well after touching a bottle. However many of those who abuse it may be injecting heroin and, as such, needles and syringes may be a normal part of their lifestyle, raising the possibility of needle stick injuries.

Q. What else do I need to know?

A. As a heroin substitute, Methadone can be legitimately prescribed to heroin addicts who sometimes trade it for heroin, or sell it in order to buy heroin. Sometimes persons abusing Methadone scratch off or deface the label and any such medicine bottles with torn labels should attract close scrutiny.

[2] CLASS B

2.i Amphetamine *[Common name]*
Speed, Whizz, Billy or Uppers *[Street names]*
Amphetamine Sulphate *[Proper name – used for wording a charge]*

Q. What is Amphetamine?
A. Amphetamines are syn-
thetic powders available in
tablet, capsule and powder
form, sometimes in combination
with other drugs to form a
cocktail. The tablets and capsules take many forms, but the
powder is normally white (though it can come
in pink), with white or orange-brown 'lumps' present. It is most
commonly distributed in 'paper wraps', a do-it-yourself type of
envelope, about one inch by half an inch, folded to safeguard
the contents.

Q. How is it abused?
A. Amphetamine can be taken orally, sniffed, smoked, or injected. Dissolving it in water and injecting it is the most common
method for heavy, regular users.

Q. What are its effects?
A. Amphetamines stimulate the nervous system to
increase energy, alertness and confidence, allowing
long periods without sleep. Adverse reactions include
loss of appetite, mood swings, aggression, insomnia
or disturbed sleep, exhaustion and uncomfortable
itching.

Q. What danger does it present to me?
A. Given that many amphetamine users inject the
drug, there is a high risk of needle stick injury, and
the associated aggression exhibited by users can pose
a physical threat to those coming in contact with
them.

Q. What else do I need to know?
A. Amphetamine is sometimes referred to as the poor man's cocaine and remains extremely popular with party goers and those who attend raves. It has a distinctive pungent ammonia smell, something akin to cat urine and once smelled is never forgotten. **(Remember though that vigorous sniffing of any substance should be avoided nor should substances ever be tasted.)**

Note: Ephedrine

Be aware that the drug Ephedrine, which is **not** controlled, is sometimes substituted knowingly or unknowingly for amphetamine. In such a case the Criminal Attempts Act 1981 may, in some circumstances, be a useful substitute, when the full offence cannot be proved.

2.ii Cannabis / Cannabis Resin *[Common name]*

Dope, Blow, Hash, Pot, Grass, Spliff, Shit *[Street names]*

Cannabis / Cannabis Resin *[Proper names – the wording of the charge must state whether the substance is cannabis or cannabis resin]*

Q. What is cannabis?

> A. Cannabis remains the most commonly abused controlled drug. It is almost always smoked, though it can, like any herb, be used in cooking, stews, cakes etc, or drunk as a tea. There are four forms:

▶ **Cannabis plant** – Cannabis Sativa is a bushy plant easily cultivated in the UK. It can easily be recognised because it has an odd number of serrated leaves (three, five, seven) on each stem of the plant. Depending upon its maturity, it is often found in warm, light places, such as window sills or, in the case of germinating seeds or small seedlings, even airing cupboards equipped with lighting strips and mirrors. When harvested, it often takes the form of dry, green leaves, which could be mistaken for culinary herbs.

▶ **Herbal cannabis** – is the imported version of the cannabis plant and, as such, is usually stronger and darker in colour, sometimes brown with the oval shaped (hemp) seeds present.

▶ **Cannabis resin** – is a resin scraped from the cannabis plant and compressed into blocks, varying in size from a house brick to a 'Victory V' lozenge. Its exotic name reflects its colour and country of origin, eg Pakistani Black, Lebanese Gold.

▶ **Cannabis oil** *(See note overleaf)*

Q. How is it abused?
A. The customary way of using cannabis is by smoking it in 'reefers' or 'joints', which are essentially home made cigarettes combining cannabis in its various forms with tobacco. Because cannabis burns at a high temperature it is likely to burn the lips of the user. To prevent this a 'widget', in the form of cardboard, is constructed from a cigarette paper packet or similar, to act as a filter. Such filters are commonly called 'roach ends'.

Q. What are its effects?
A. Cannabis can create a feeling of euphoria, often accompanied by talkativeness, incoherent giggling and fits of laughter. However, it can also cause a lack of co-ordination, confusion, disorientation and psychological dependency.

Q. What danger does it present to me?
A. Cannabis use can often progress to, or run parallel with, harder drug abuse, bringing with it the associated risks.

Q. What else do I need to know?
A. Small deals of cannabis come in various forms depending upon the type. Bush (the plant) usually comes in polythene or paper bags, while resin is likely to be packaged in Clingfilm in a variety of shapes, from slabs, to 'Oxo cube' sized cakes to matchstick like strips. All cannabis, of whatever type, has a distinctive sweet scented smell, hence the use of masking agents such as sticks or patchouli oil, a perfume from an Indian herb.

Note: Cannabis oil

Cannabis oil is a concentrated liquid form of the drug. It is expensive to buy and comes in small bottles, into which a pointed object is dipped and stroked along the length of a tailor-made cigarette which is then simply smoked.

Note: Super cannabis

'Skunk weed', so called because of its strong pungent smell, is an enhanced strain of cannabis and is becoming increasingly popular and more prominent on the drug scene. It commands a high street price, though legally it is the same as normal strength cannabis.

[3] CLASS C

3.i Temazepam *[Common name]*

[Street names] **Wobbly Eggs, Jellies, Rugby Ball**

Temazepam *[Proper name – used for wording charge]*

Q. What is Temazepam?
A. Temazepam is a prescribed tranquilliser. It is popularly abused and comes in three forms, as a small white tablet, a soft, oval shaped half inch capsule, either yellow or green in colour, or as a hard, oval shaped yellow green capsule. It is also available as a syrup.

Q. How is it abused?
A. The most popular form of abuse is by injection, whereby the capsule is warmed to liquefy it before being pierced by a hypodermic needle and drawn into the syringe, then injected, to provide a heroin-like 'rush'.

Q. What are its effects?

A. The drug depresses alertness and mental activity, and through lowering inhibitions may produce aggression in the abuser. Often, when taken in high doses, it creates drowsiness and sleep. The effect lasts between three to six hours.

Q. What danger does it present to me?

A. Because the drug is injected it exposes both users and non-users to disease and needle stick injuries, added to which there is the possibility of aggressive behaviour.

Q. What else do I need to know?

A. Temazepam is particularly popular amongst heroin users who may use it as a temporary fix until they are able to 'score' the real thing.

Note: Availability

From 1 January 1996, the most commonly abused form of Temazepam, the gel filled capsules known as 'wobbly eggs', 'jellies' or 'rugby balls', have no longer been prescribable by general practitioners under the National Health Service. However they remain available on private prescription with other forms of the drug still available under the National Health Service.

This decision was taken by the Government after concern about growing abuse of the capsules. However because of the demand for Temazepam amongst abusers it will no doubt continue to be used illicitly, probably by injecting, whereby the tablets will be crushed, mixed into a liquid and prepared as a solution for intravenous use. In an effort to overcome the non-availability of capsules, capsules containing the drug have have been 'illicitly' manufactured in an attempt to meet the demands of users

Home Office Circular No65/1995 provides further details of offences and requirements in respect of Temazepam.

3.ii Temgesic *[Common name]*

Temmies *[Street name]*

Buprenorphine *[Proper name – used for wording charge]*

Q. What is Temgesic?
A. This is a prescribed painkiller which is now a primary drug of abuse as a heroin substitute. It comes in a blister pack bearing the Dettol sword trademark containing 'pop out' white tablets about a quarter inch in diameter.

Q. How is it abused?
A. It is invariably crushed, dissolved and injected to provide the much desired 'rush'.

Q. What are its effects?
A. Its effects and side effects mirror those of heroin *(see page 11).*

Q. What danger does it present to me?
A. As with heroin users, those who abuse 'Temmies' may share needles, increasing the risk of disease from needle stick injuries.

Q. What else do I need to know?
A. The abuse of Temgesic tends to be local in character, being restricted to specific areas of the country

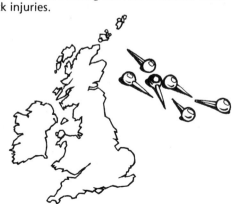

3.iii Anabolic Steroids *[Common name]*

Steroids, Gear, Juice, Stuff, Roids *[Street names – for the term used for wording a charge, be guided by information provided by the forensic scientist. See also Class C Drugs listed in Schedule 2, Misuse of Drugs Act 1971, page 37.]*

Q. What are Anabolic Steroids?
A. There are many varied compounds which come under the term 'steroid'. However, those generally abused are the anabolic steroids, which are used by body-builders and athletes to enhance their physique and performance.

Q. How are they abused?
A. Steroids can be taken orally in tablet form or by intramuscular injection of the drug which is drawn by syringe from a small glass phial or larger multidose bottles. They should never be injected into a vein.

Q. What are their effects?
A. Among the physical symptoms likely to be experienced by the user is an increase in size and weight, producing well-developed muscles. Acne may well appear on the face and upper body of those using the drug coupled with changes in sexual characteristics and an obsession with supplements and nutrition.

Q. What dangers does it present to me?
A. Because a method of use is by injection, needle stick injuries present a real threat of spreading diseases associated with intravenous drug misuse. Also of concern is the anxiety and aggression that can be induced by taking steroids.

Q. What else do I need to know?

A. Parliament has now approved an order, the Misuse of Drugs Act 1971 (Modification) Order 1996, which brings 48 anabolic steroids and six other similar drugs under the controls of the Misuse of Drugs Act 1971. The order, which adds the 54 substances to the list of Class 'C' drugs, was enforceable from September 1, 1996.

See Schedule 2 of the Misuse of Drugs Act 1971)
See Home Office Circular No 29/1996

These controls are aimed at those who unlawfully supply anabolic steroids and, accordingly, people who without authority produce, supply, posses with intent to supply or who import or export them with intent to supply, will be guilty of offences. However no offence is committed by those who simply possess them or those who import or export the drug for personal use.

[4] MISCELLANEOUS

Misc

4.i Magic Mushrooms [*Common name*]
Magic Mushroom, Liberty Cap
[*Street names*]

PSILOCIN [*Proper name –
used for wording a charge*]

Q. What is a Magic Mushroom?
A. Magic mushrooms (Psilocybe) are
found in the late summer in damp grassy
areas. They contain an hallucinogenic
compound called psilocybin which, when ingested, is converted
into the Class A drug, Psilocin, which has a similar effect to LSD.
In fact, the user experiences the effects even quicker than with
LSD, but the trips are of shorter duration.

Q. How is it abused?

A. Picked in great quantities magic mushrooms can be eaten in their natural state.
Sometimes they are dried and eaten or
made into tea, soup or added to 'home
brew' – they can even be included in cook-
ing. Alternatively they can be dried,
ground into powder, mixed with tobacco
and smoked.

Q. What are its effects?
A. The LSD-like effects include
a feeling of euphoria, detachment and visual distortions and
hallucinations of colour and
movement. Adverse effects
include high blood pressure,
increased heart rate, stomach
upsets and, subsequently, a
hangover. They can create a
psychological rather than physical dependence.

Q. What danger does it present to me?
A. There may be dangers in handling them, depending upon their concentration, but the main danger comes from the abusers themselves, whose behaviour when under the influence of the drug may be unpredictable.

Q. What else do I need to know?
A. This is a very important question, given the legal status of magic mushrooms which, in their natural state, do not amount to an offence under the Misuse of Drugs Act 1971 in relation to growing, possession and use. However when 'altered by the hand of man' ie, prepared by drying or freezing, cooked or powdered etc, an offence is committed. Similarly, supplying frozen, dried or powdered mushrooms would amount to supplying Psilocin, a Class A drug, listed in Schedule 2 to the Act *(see page 35)*.

Comment

The decided case, *Hodder and Another v DPP* ([1990] Crim LR 261), may help to clarify the position in respect of magic mushrooms. During a raid on premises, drug squad officers found bags of magic mushrooms stored in a refrigerator. Examination by a forensic scientist revealed that the mushrooms contained an ester of Psilocin – a Class A drug listed in Part 1 of Schedule 2 to the Act. Hodder argued that the mushrooms must be processed before they could be used to create hallucinations. Because the mushrooms were packed, and labelled, the court held they came with the meaning included in para 5 of Part I of Schedule 2 to the Act.

Misc

4.ii Solvents *[Common name]*

Includes

adhesive – aerosols – paint lacquer – thinners – butane gas – lighter fuel – nail varnish – petrol – shoe polish – typewriter correcting fluid – hair-spray – pain relief spray – marker pens – de-icer – rubber solution – deoderant spray – metal polish – and many, many more.

Intoxicating substances *[Proper name – used for wording a charge – see note overleaf]*

Q. What are solvents?
A. In essence, all of these intoxicating substances are common everyday products which are 'sniffable'.

Q. How are they abused?
A. There are many ways of inhaling these substances. Some are sniffed from bags, a practice called 'huffing'; some aerosols and gases are sprayed directly into the mouth; some, such as thinners or typewriter fluid, are sniffed from a cloth, rag, or even a paper handkerchief.

Q. What are their effects?
A. The effects are like those of drunkenness caused by alcohol, though swifter and of shorter duration, hence the tendency to keep sniffing to remain high. Some abusers become drunk very quickly and may experience hallucinations. Signs and symptoms include dilated pupils, sore and runny nose, cracked lips, excessive saliva, pimples around the nose and mouth, unsteadiness and a vacant expression, poor co-ordination, lethargy and memory loss.

Q. What danger do they present to me?
A. The substances themselves are more inconvenient than dangerous, posing problems of disposal, etc. The danger lies in the behaviour of the abuser who can be unruly, offensive and difficult to handle.

Many of the abusers are children or young persons who often go to out-of-the-way places to practise their habit, sometimes employing highly dangerous methods and running the risk of death. These dangers include:

▶ **suffocation** from having placed the head inside the plastic bag, or via a swelling of the throat when spraying directly into the mouth
▶ **asphyxiation** from choking on their own vomit
▶ **burns** from a combination of smoking and the highly flammable nature of the substances
▶ **injury or death** from the effects of hallucinations, intoxication or risk-taking, often in dangerous environments, such as old buildings, canals, or secluded places.

Many of these abusers are highly vulnerable and would benefit from assistance from people working together using a multi-agency approach.

Note: Possible offences

While the abuser commits no specific offence relating to possessing the substance, any number of offences could be committed due to the effects of inhalation, including public order, motoring offences etc.

Section 1 of the Intoxicating Substances (Supply) Act 1985, recognises the importance of protecting potential users from a ready supply of such substances. Under this legislation it is an offence to supply or offer to supply any such substance to someone under 18, or whom the supplier knows or has reason to believe to be under 18, or any person acting for a person under that age whom the supplier knows or has reasonable course to believe is acting as such, if the supplier knows or has reasonable cause to believe that the substance or its fumes are likely to be inhaled by a person under 18. In practice, proving the degree of guilty knowledge by the supplier concerning either the purchaser, the go-between or the user can prove difficult.

The Intoxicating Substances (Supply) Act 1985 applies in England, Wales and Northern Ireland.*

S   * In Scotland prosecution is under the common law whereby knowingly supplying solutions for 'sniffing' is liable to even more severe penalties.

[5] OTHERS

There are a number of other substances which are abused and of concern to all those engaged in drug-related work, despite the fact that they are not yet subject to control; though most are under consideration by the Government, so watch for changes in their legal status. For your information we have described a few of the most popular 'legal', but abused, substances.

5.i GBH

GBH (Gamma-Hydroxybutyrate or Sodium Oxybate) is a colourless, odourless liquid sold in small plastic bottles at dances and raves. It produces euphoria, breaks down inhibitions and may cause mild hallucinations, hence it is sometimes called 'liquid ecstasy', though given its potential side effects the name GBH (grievous bodily harm) may be more appropriate.

5.ii 'Kit Kat' – Ketamine

Kit Kat also known as Special K, Super K, and Vitamin K, is in reality Ketamine (Ketamine Hydrochloride), an anaesthetic which comes in ampoules, tablets, capsules and powder and can be injected, swallowed or sniffed. It produces an 'out of body experience', a feeling of floating free, hallucinations which can appear real, an increase in energy and feelings of aggression. As with LSD, users can experience flashbacks.

5.iii Khat

Khat is the bark of a leafy green plant which is sometimes imported to Britain from East Africa and Arabia. It can be chewed or brewed as a tea and contains the mild stimulant, cathaedalis, which is not a controlled drug. It produces a feeling of euphoria accompanied by talkativeness followed by calm.

It brings with it risks of mouth infection, even cancer, probable heart trouble and the loss of sex-drive in males.

5.iv Poppers

Poppers (Amyl-nitrate) are a heart stimulant sold often in sex shops, as a liquid in small bottles, with names such as 'Rush' and 'Liquid Gold'. The vapour is inhaled to increase heart rate and produces a flushing effect, a brief rush, and heightens sexual arousal. It can cause dizziness and blackouts.

[6] APPENDIX A – POWERS OF ARREST

Q. What are the relevant Powers of Arrest?

A. To assist officers in determining their arrest powers we have linked the main offences in relation to drugs together with their power of arrest.

Offence (under the Misuse of Drugs Act 1971)	Power of Arrest
*Unlawful importation or exportation (s 3)	ARRESTABLE OFFENCE
Unlawful production (s 4(2))	
Unlawful supply (s 4(3))	
Unlawful possession (Class A or B) (s 5(2))	
Possession with intent to supply (s 5(3))	
Cultivation of cannabis (s 6(2))	
Controlled drugs on premises (s 8)	
Activities relating to opium	
Smoke, use, frequent place, posses pipes and utensils (s 9)	
Unlawful possession (s 5(2)) (Class C)	GENERAL ARREST CONDITIONS
Supply drugs preparation, or drugs administration kits (s 9A(i))	

* *Section 3, Misuse of Drugs Act 1971, provides for unlawful importation/exportation under the Customs Management Act 1979.*

S The term arrestable offence is not used in Scottish law. Scots officers should refer to s 24 of the Misuse of Drugs Act 1971 which states: 'A constable may arrest without warrant a person who has committed or whom the constable with reasonable cause suspects to have committed an offence under the Act if: (a) he, with reasonable cause, believes that that person will abscond unless arrested; or (b) the name and address of that person are unknown to, and cannot be ascertained by, him; or (c) he is not satisfied that a name and address furnished by that person as his name and address are true.'

In addition Scots officers may be able to use their more liberal common law powers of arrest, if the circumstances allow.

[B] Important drug schedules

This section features the important drug legislation schedules. The key schedule to the Misuse of Drugs Act 1971 is Schedule 2, which lists all the substances controlled under the Act, categorising them in one of three classes (A, B or C) depending upon their potential harm, which is reflected in the penalties and hence police powers (ie arrestable offences). The latest amended schedule currently available is detailed below. *See also a brief explanation of the Misuse of Drugs Regulations 1985, as to what purpose they serve (page 39).*

SCHEDULE 2 MISUSE OF DRUGS ACT 1971

Class A Drugs

Acetorphine
Alfentanil
Allylprodine
Alphacetylmethadol
Alphameprodine
Alphamethadol
Alphaprodine
Anileridine
Benzethidine
Benzylmorphine
  (3-benzylmorphine)
Betacetylmethadol
Betameprodine
Betamethadol
Betaprodine
Bezitramide
Bufotenine
Cannabinol
  (except where contained in
  cannabis or cannabis resin)
Cannabinol derivatives
Carfentanil
Clonitazene
Coca leaf
Cocaine

Desomorphine
Dextromoramide
Diamorphine
Diampromide
Diethylthiamutene
Difenoxin
  (1-(3-cyano-3,
  3-diphenylpropyl-4-phenyl
  piperidine-4-Carboxylic acid
Dihydrocodeine
  O-Carboxymethyloxime
Dihyrdomorphine
Dimenoxadole
Dimephaptanol
Dimethylthiambutene
Dioxaphetyl butyrate
Diphenoxylate
Dipipanone
Drotebanol
  (3, 4-dimethoxy-17-
  methylmorphinan 6, 14-diol)
Ecgonine
  (and any derivative of ecgonine
  which is convertible to ecgonine
  or to cocaine)
Ethylmethylthiambutene

Eticyclidine
Etonitazene
Etorphine
Etoxeridine
Fentanyl
Furethidine
Hydrocodone
Hydromorphinol
Hydromorphone
Hydroxypethidine
N-Hydroxytenamphetamine
    (N-Hydroxy MDA)
Isomethadone
Ketobemidone
Levomethorphan
Levomoramide
Levophenacylmorphan
Levorphanol
Lofentanil
Lysergamide
Lysergide
    and other N-alkyl derivatives
    of lysergamide
Mescaline
Metazocine
Methadone
Methadyl acetate
Methylaminorex
Methyldesorphine
Methyldihydromorphine
    (6-methyldihydromorphine)
Metopon
Morpheridine
Morphine
Morphine methobromide
    morphine N-oxide and other
    pentavalent nitrogen morphine
    derivatives

Myrophine
Nicomorphine
    (3, 6-dinicotinoyl-morphine)
Noracymethadol
Norlevorphanol
Normethadone
Normorphine
Norpipanone
Opium –
    whether raw, prepared or
    medicinal
Oxycodone
Ocymorphone
Pethidine
Phenadoxone
Phenampromide
Phenaxocine
Phencyclidine
Phenomorphan
Phenoperidine
Piminodine
Piritramide
    Concentrate of poppy straw
Proheptazine
Properidine
    (1-methyl-4-phenyl-piperidine-4-
    carboxylic acid isopropyl ester)
Psilocin
Racemethorphan
Racemoramide
Racemorphan
Rolicyclidine
Sufentanil
Tenocyclidine
Thebacon
Thebaine
Tilidate
Trimeperidine

Class B Drugs

Acetyldihydrodcodeine
Amphetamine
Cannabis and cannabis resin
Codeine
Cannabis

   (except in the expression
   Cannabis Resin) means any plant
   of the genus Cannabis or any
   part of any such plant (by
   whatever name designated)
   except that it does not include
   cannabis resin or any of the
   following products after
   separation from the rest of the
   plant, namely:
(a) mature stalk of any such plant,
(b) fibre produced from mature stalk
   of any such plant, and
(c) seed of any such plant.
   (Note: This definition of cannabis
   in s 52 of the Criminal Law Act
   1977 replaces the definition of
   cannabis in s 37(1) of the Misuse
   of Drugs Act 1971)

Dihydrocodeine
Ethylmorphine
   (3-ethylmorphine)
Glutethimide
Lefetamine
Mecloqualone
Methaqualone
Methylamphetamine
Methylphenidate
Methylphenobarbitone
Nicocodine
Nicodicodine
   (6-nicotinoyldihydrocodeine)
Norcodeine
Pentazocine
Phenmetrazine
Pholcodine
Propiram
Quinalbarbitone

Authors' note to schedule 2

There are more complex compounds, esters, ethers and salts which will require specialist scientific knowledge. We suggest that you seek expert advice and refer to the full schedule contained in the Misuse of Drugs Act 1971.

Class C Drugs

Alprazolam
Benzphetamine
Bromazepam
Buprenorphine
Camazepam
Cathine
Cathinone
Chlorodiazepoxide
Chlorphentermine
Clobazam
Clonazepam
Clorazepic acid
Clotiazepam
Cloxazoam
Delorazepam
Dextropropoxyphene
Diazepam
Diethylpropion
Estazolam
Ethchlorvynol
Ethinamate
Ethyl loflazepate
Fencamfamine
Fenethylline
Fenproporex
Fludiazepam
Flurazepam
Halazepam
Haloxazolam

Ketazolam
Loprazolam
Lorazepam
Lormetazepam
Mazindol
Medazepam
Mefenorex
Mephentermine
Meprobamate
Methyprylone
Midazolam
Nimetazepam
Nitrazepam
Noriazepam
Oxazepam
Oxazolam
Pemoline
Phendimetrazine
Phentermine
Pinazepam
Pipradrol
Prazepam
Propylhexedire
Pyrovaleron
Temazepam
Tetrazepam
Triazolam
N-Ethylamphetamine

Class C Drugs as included by the Misuse of Drugs Act 1971 (Modification) Order 1996

Atamestane
Bolandiol
Boiasterone
Bolazine
Boldenone
Bolenol
Bolmantalate
Calusterone
 4. Chloromethandienone
Clostebol
Drostanolone
Enestebol
Epitiostanol
Ethyloestrenol
Fluoxymesterone
Formebolone
Furazabol
Mebolazine
Mepitiostane
Mesabolone
Mestanolone
Mesterolone
Methandienone
Methandriol
Methenolone
Methyltestosterone
Meribolone

Mibolerone
Nandrolone
Norboletone
Norclostebol
Norethandrolone
Ovandrotone
Oxymesterone
Oxymetholone
Oxabolone
Oxandrolone
Prasterone
Propetandrol
Quinbolone
Roxibolone
Silandrone
Stanolone
Stanozolol
Stenbolone
Testosterone
Thiomesterone
Trenbolone
 Chorionic Gonadotrophin (HCG)
 Clenbuterol
 Non-human chorionic
 gonadotrphin
Somatotropin
Somatrem
Somatropin

Authors' note to schedule 2

There are more complex compounds, esters, ethers and salts which will require specialist scientific knowledge. We suggest that you seek expert advice and refer to the full schedule contained in the Misuse of Drugs Act 1971

SCHEDULE 3
MISUSE OF DRUGS REGULATIONS 1985

There are certain classes of people who, in 'the course of their business' are authorised to possess, supply, produce and prescribe controlled drugs, eg general practitioners and pharmacists.

The Misuse of Drugs Regulations 1985 provide the necessary controls and restrictions which apply to various substances. These are categorised into five schedules to the regulations. Controls and restrictions on substances are based on the schedule in which they are accommodated.

For example, Temazepam is controlled as a Class C drug under the Misuse of Drugs Act 1971 and was, until 1996, within schedule four of the Misuse of Drugs Regulations 1985. Because Temazepam was becoming a real problem in the way it was being abused the drug was moved to schedule 3 where it is now subject to more stringent conditions concerning security at pharmacists'. Licenses are now required for importation and exportation of the drug and simple possession of Temazepam without authority has been made an offence *(see Home Office Circular 65/1995)*.

You will see from this example how the regulations work and how controls concerning records, prescriptions and safe custody requirements are considered and implemented. Once the changes become law the Home Office Circular is put out to chief officers and those connected with the Criminal Justice System for information.

It may be necessary for you to refer to the regulations in the course of certain investigations or seek advice on them from specialists.

Chapter 3

DRUGS SAFETY

INTRODUCTION

This chapter looks closely at the action that should be taken when dealing with drug and solvent-related illness and provides information intended to safeguard you during contact with drug users who may present a high risk factor.

During the course of drug-related inquiries, or perhaps even while simply carrying out routine police duties, you may be called upon to administer first aid to someone who has overdosed. Hospital accident and emergency units will confirm that such incidents occur all too frequently. Abusers not only place themselves at risk by overdosing, but face a real threat of exposure to one of the viruses which can affect drug users, particularly those who inject or who associate with intravenous users.

Before reading the following pages consider these questions carefully.

> ◗ If called upon to render first aid to some-
> one who has overdosed are you confident
> that you could help?

> ◗ Are you aware of the threat posed by
> particular substances of abuse?

> ◗ Are you yourself protected against the
> type of infections that are associated with
> drug abuse?

> ◗ Do you know how to go about safe-
> guarding yourself against the viruses that
> exist?

To assist you we have broken down the risks associated with drug and solvent abuse into two areas – the risk to you and the risk to the users. Broadly the chapter is divided as overleaf:

[A] Drugs and associated risks

The following check list highlights the risk factors connected to the more popular substances of abuse. Remember, some of these risks can affect you by way of transference through careless handling or lack of care when searching. You will see that the risks do not always exist because of the substance itself, although the body can be poisoned, but occur because of the method of abuse.

[1] INJECTING

The most hazardous way of abusing drugs is by injecting as you will see.

Method of abuse	Risks to user	Substance
Injecting (Either by re-using or sharing needles/ injecting equipment)	Blood Infections such as Hepatitis, HIV or AIDS	Cocaine Heroin Amphetamine Temazepam Steroids, etc
Orally, or by being absorbed through the skin	Recurring hallucinations (flashbacks), Dizziness	LSD
Orally, sniffed or smoked	Reduced resistance to disease. Prolonged itching skin irritation	Amphetamine

See also chapter 2 which details the risk associated with each of the major drugs of abuse.

Substances that are injected fall mainly into three group:

> ▶ opiates (such as heroin)
> ▶ tranquillisers (such as Temazepam)
> ▶ stimulants (such as amphetamines and cocaine).

Q. Why do people inject?

A. Injecting gets the drug into the blood stream quickly, ensuring that some is routed immediately to the brain to produce the desired 'rush'. As a result the effects of the substance are intensified, adding to the risks that already exist. Despite these risks, those who inject find the custom of injecting as vital to their needs as the actual drug. The 'rush' felt by the body as the drug travels round the user's blood stream to the brain is quite often the initial driving force behind injecting. Once a tolerance to the drug develops, larger doses are required to get the desired effect, until the body finally needs the substance simply to function normally. By this stage many users become dependent on the drug and will experience little effect other than the 'rush' of injecting; followed by sleepiness, hyper-activity or simply normality, depending on the substance.

Q. What are the main dangers to health associated with injecting?

A. HIV and AIDS; Hepatitis (particularly Hepatitis B and C; other risks (ie overdose; abscesses; inflamed veins; septicemia; gangrene and other bodily damage).

[2] HIV AND AIDS

You will have noticed these terms documented as risk factors when drugs are injected. They deserve particular attention in this section as you can do much to reduce the risk of contracting HIV or Hepatitis.

Q. Are HIV and AIDS the same thing?
A. No. HIV (Human Immunodeficiency Virus) is just that – a virus which weakens the immune system which protects the body's defences so it is unable to fight off certain infections. AIDS can then develop from HIV.

Q. How do you get HIV?
A. HIV is carried in blood and other body fluids, also breast milk, cerebro-spinal fluid and amniotic fluid – such as semen or vaginal fluids – of people who are infected. The virus can only be passed on to other people if those fluids get into their body. HIV may be transmitted through:

▶ unprotected sexual intercourse (anal or vaginal).
▶ sharing injecting equipment and getting infected blood into the bloodstream
▶ blood transfusions where infected blood is received
▶ surgical procedures, or where infected blood splashes into the eye, mouth or onto broken skin, such as a cut or wound
▶ between mother and baby – during the course of pregnancy and birth, or breast feeding.

Comment

Health educationalists believe that the level of the virus contained in saliva, blister fluid and tears is insufficient to be infectious and so far as we know there have been no proven cases of HIV infection from these body fluids.

Comment

With HIV, while needle stick injuries are not a common route of infection, they are a possible route, so take extreme care when dealing with injecting drug abusers and recoveries.

Q. What can I do to protect myself from accidental exposure to HIV?
A. Normal social or day-to-day work contact with people living with HIV presents no risk of transmitting the virus. Nor is their ability to work affected. In the event of accidents or contact with body fluids, take the same precautions with HIV as you would with any other infection and apply the same high standard of good infection control.

▶ Make sure sores and cuts are protected with waterproof plasters.
▶ When handling blood or other body substances during searching or bagging evidence, or clearing up spillage, make sure gloves are worn together with other protective clothing.
▶ Dispose of needles and 'works' safely in clearly marked puncture proof containers (but note the need to preserve evidence).
▶ Make sure, when clearing up spillages of blood or any other body substance, such as those found in cells or on charge room counters, that:
(i) absorbent cloth or paper are used to soak up spillages; and
(ii) use hot water and detergent to clean up the spillage; then
(iii) use good quality bleach with hot water to clean the affected area;
(iv) dispose of the cloths and paper wipes in a sealed polythene bag; then
(v) wash your hands.

Note: Safety in transit

When forwarding evidence containing high risk items to others involved in the investigative process, warn them of the risk by using 'Health Hazard Tape' clearly displayed on each package.

Q. So what is AIDS?

A. As explained, AIDS is what can develop in some people, who have HIV, when the immune system breaks down.

AIDS stands for:

> ❯ Acquired – developing over time (as in acquired taste)
>
> ❯ Immune – the defence mechanism of the body
>
> ❯ Deficiency – the body's defence mechanism is absent
>
> ❯ Syndrome – a combination of infections and illnesses can occur

Because of the body's inability to fight off infection and illness, a significant number of those with AIDS develop serious infections of the lungs, central nervous system, digestive system and skin. Certain forms of cancer are particularly common among sufferers.

[3] HEPATITIS

The viral infection known as Hepatitis is particularly risky for drug users and those involved in drug-related inquiries where contact with injecting equipment is likely. This section seeks to provide an awareness of this blood-borne virus and help individuals to recognise when they may be placed at risk.

Q. What is Hepatitis?
Hepatitis is a viral infection of the liver and there are three main types – A, B and C. The ones which most often affect drug abusers are Hepatitis B and C.

[3.i] Hepatitis B

Q. What does Hepatitis B do?
A. Those who contract this particular type of Hepatitis may become seriously ill and suffer permanent damage of the liver. It may even result in death although most people recover fully within about six months. Some of those who recover will continue to be infectious to others without displaying the symptoms common to the virus.

Q. What are the symptoms?
A. Symptoms may include:
▶ tiredness, aching joints and muscles, flu-like symptoms and generally feeling ill
▶ jaundice – where the skin and whites of the eyes turn yellow
▶ pale stools and darker urine
▶ pain in the back or side (in the liver)
▶ no desire to eat, a feeling of nausea, stomach pains and vomiting.

Q. How can a person catch Hepatitis B?
A. It can be passed from person to person through contact with blood, semen, vaginal or cervical fluids or breast milk. This can be done in the following ways:

▶ having unprotected vaginal or anal sexual intercourse, or oral sex
▶ sharing razors or toothbrushes
▶ when injecting drugs, sharing equipment
▶ mother-to-baby during pregnancy
▶ mother-to-baby when breast feeding
▶ injection or needle stick injuries from contaminated equipment (body piercing, tattooing, or acupuncture)
▶ infected blood or body fluids coming into contact with open cuts and sores or getting into the mouth or eyes.

Comment

A blood test is the only way that Hepatitis B can be diagnosed and the tests can reveal if you have previously had, or if you currently have, the virus.

Q. How can a person avoid catching Hepatitis B?

A. By being cautious and in particular by:

▶ not sharing equipment when injecting drugs
▶ practising safer sex (using a condom for vaginal, anal and oral sex and exploring alternative methods of love-making)
▶ never sharing toothbrushes and shaving equipment
▶ ensuring that only registered practitioners carry out any body piercing, acupuncture or tattooing;
▶ protecting open cuts or sores from spilled blood or body fluid
▶ being immunised against Hepatitis B (see advice overleaf)
▶ handling and disposing of 'works' and other injecting equipment safely.

Comment

Remember to dispose of 'works' and 'sharps' safely in approved containers and cover any abrasions or cuts with a suitable waterproof dressing. If needle stick injuries are received, report them as soon as possible to your occupational health officer, GP or hospital, as treatment may be necessary.

Q. How do I go about protecting myself by immunisation?
A. You may have an occupational health officer in your Force who will supply correct information regarding medical and health and safety issues and will give advice on how to safeguard yourself. If you do not have an occupational health officer in post, then contact your Force medical officer (police surgeon) or general practitioner who will help.

Basically a course of injections is given over a period of six months, after which booster doses may be required to ensure immunity. The vaccination is effective and safe although a blood test at the conclusion of the course of injections is taken to check that the person is properly protected. You will also need to have further tests over the years to ensure that you remain fully immune. Immunity is not, however, guaranteed.

Note: Continuing risks

▶ Carriers of Hepatitis 'B' risk passing on the virus even before they develop symptoms.

▶ Some carriers display no symptoms of the virus but are infectious to other people.

▶ Although most people with the virus recover completely within six months some remain infectious while having no symptoms.

▶ Serious liver damage may result from Hepatitis B.

[3.ii] Hepatitis C

Q. What is Hepatitis C?

A. The Hepatitis C virus was identified in 1988, and is found in blood. It is similar to other viral infections in that time will elapse between exposure to Hepatitis C and any subsequent symptoms or illness. Symptoms are often general in nature and could easily be attributed to a number of illnesses. Indeed, infected people may not show any symptoms at all and the only way you will find out if you have the Hepatitis C virus is to have a blood test.

Note: Dried blood

The virus has the ability to survive in dried blood outside the body for many days.

Q. What are the symptoms of Hepatitis C?

A. Two phases exist in respect of this infection

▶ **Active phase**

Signs and symptoms can take up to four months to appear after exposure to infection. During this period there may be no symptoms at all or very mild signs may develop. These may include:

- loss of appetite (particularly with respect to fatty foods, eggs and alcohol)
- tiredness/fatigue – aches and pains
- 'flu- like symptoms – stomach discomfort – nausea – mild jaundice – depression

About 30 per cent of those suffering from acute Hepatitis C recover completely while remaining sufferers go on to develop long term (chronic) Hepatitis C infection.

▶ Chronic phase

Symptoms of chronic Hepatitis C are not always too severe and may only be apparent as a mild, on-going form of the virus although sufferers who overwork or are stressed may show more intense symptoms. Those with chronic Hepatitis C can go on to develop cirrhosis of the liver, where the organ becomes scarred, or liver cancer. About five per cent of people with chronic Hepatitis C may overcome the infection, although no explanation can be given for this.

Comment

The diseases caused by Hepatitis C are serious for many people and can prove fatal.

Q. How do you catch Hepatitis C?

A. When infected blood from a person comes into contact with the bloodstream of another person. A minute amount of infected blood is sufficient to catch the disease which can be spread by drug users sharing needles or syringes and other equipment used for injecting. It does not matter what drugs are being used as the virus is passed on through blood.

Comment

Hepatitis C is very common among UK drug abusers who inject and it may be possible for 50 per cent of these to have chronic Hepatitis C infection.

Note

Ways to protect against Hepatitis C are constantly being researched and inquiries regarding this particular strain of the virus should be directed to those medically qualified.

Comment

Never make assumptions. You are unlikely to be able to tell simply by looking at someone whether that person is infected by one or more of the viruses we have covered. The basic rule is always play safe and treat those you come into contact with cautiously and reduce the risk of exposing yourself to infection. Remember to always safeguard yourself, and be alert for techniques adopted by some drug abusers to harm you – biting, for example, or the strategic positioning of needles on car seats or taped to door handles.

[4] OTHER RISKS

Other dangers can also arise for drug users
from injecting drugs:

Overdose (poisoning)	Some may be attempted suicides, but most are accidental, because the user is unaware of the purity or otherwise of the substance and has no knowledge of how or with what substance it has been mixed (adulterated)
Abscesses or inflamed veins	Caused by constant injecting under unhygenic conditions.
Septicemia	Infection in the blood.
Gangrene	Death of tissue caused usually by a micro-organism (Clostridium) which can be caused by needle sharing.
Bodily damage (Necrosis)	Blockage of the blood supply caused by using crushed tablets and other substances (not intended to be injected) causing loss of limbs.

Comment

Although these 'other dangers' do not present health risks to
those coming into contact with drug abusers – with the exception
of septicemia and gangrene – they are important considerations
when handling prisoners, given that the police are responsible for
their general health and welfare.

[B] First Aid

During this section we will concentrate on how you should react when faced with someone who has fallen ill through substance misuse. People who have overdosed may die if not dealt with properly and because such incidents have become more frequent it follows that the chances of your being called upon to help have also increased. Your initial basic actions may prove vital in saving lives.

[1] SOLVENT ABUSE

This is the term that is generally given to the 'sniffing' or 'inhaling' of products, often referred to as 'abusable substances' as defined in the Intoxicating Substances (Supply) Act 1985 *(see chapter 2)*. Many of these appear innocent, are often found around the home, and are potentially lethal. Once again it is extremely difficult to know what a 'sniffer' will look like, so do not be misled. Like drug abuse there are no class barriers involved and 'sniffers' come from all different backgrounds with both sexes involved and all age groups. However, the majority are male and aged between 11 and 17 years.

Q. Why do young people 'sniff'?

A. There are many reasons, including peer pressure – habit or craze in a particular local area – curiosity – boredom – developed psychological dependency – enjoyment of the high and the resulting hallucinations – cheaper than alcohol – low self-image – problems at school/home – rebellion – unable to form relationships – escape from reality – family arguments – bullying.

Q. What do people 'sniff'?

A. Pain relief spray, lighter refills, fly spray, hair lacquers and other aerosols, are abused by the user spraying it down the throat or up the nose. Some people have died moments after inhalation and others risk sudden death every time they use gas or aerosols in this way. It is believed that the gas interferes with the normal rhythm of the heart and causes it to stop suddenly. Heart failure can also result from the user being over active while 'sniffing'. Another serious cause for concern is that the gases can damage the lungs by freezing them.

Q. What do I do when I find someone in an intoxicated condition and I suspect solvents?

A. See Emergency Treatment, page 61. It is important that you act swiftly but don't get flustered because you may alarm the 'sniffer', bringing about a violent reaction which in turn may lead to heart failure.

Then:

▶ make sure the solvent or other substance is removed
▶ ensure that anything which might lead to asphyxia is removed, ie false teeth, vomit, tight clothing around the neck, food, sweets, etc
▶ allow the 'sniffer' access to plenty of fresh air
▶ try talking to the 'sniffer' and reassure him/her
▶ get professional help/call an ambulance.

In addition... if unconscious – check:

▶ that the airway is clear (ensure the tongue is not causing an obstruction)
▶ that the 'sniffer' is breathing
▶ the heartbeat of the 'sniffer', then
      – loosen clothing around the neck and chest
      – place in recovery position (on stomach) to prevent inhaling vomit
      – if breathing has ceased apply artificial ventilation (mouth-to-mouth)
      – ascertain exactly what has happened.

Comment

Protect yourself when carrying out mouth-to-mouth resuscitation by using a proper device designed for that purpose, often issued by forces as standard equipment, or blow through a cloth. Remember to clean your lips well afterwards, as corrosive substances may have been transferred onto them.

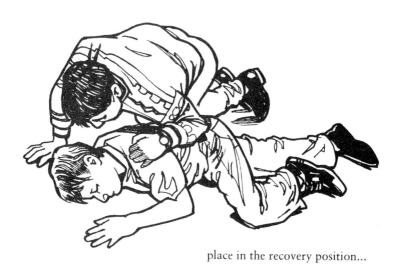

place in the recovery position...

If the 'sniffer' is conscious...

▶ be aware that the person may lose consciousness at any time, so ask what has happened
▶ keep the 'sniffer' calm and relaxed
▶ keep the 'sniffer' warm
▶ watch the 'sniffer' constantly in case he/she loses consciousness.

When the ambulance crew arrive tell them what has happened; that you suspect gas or aerosol misuse, and show them the relevant canister or container.

Comment

Remember that the user's behaviour may be unpredictable under the circumstances and you should safeguard yourself against violent reaction at all times. Ensure the surrounding area is safe before approaching an individual. You should not become a casualty.

[2] DRUGS OVERDOSE

The emergency treatment for a drugs overdose is almost identical to that required for a person who is ill through solvent abuse. Consider the following scenario:

> While walking along the street, a member of the public stops you and directs you to a nearby public toilet saying he has heard strange noises coming from one of the cubicles. When you arrive, the cubicle door is locked and you get no response from inside, but can see a pair of feet under the door. You look over the top and see a young male slumped back on the toilet seat. The youth, obviously unconscious, has blue lips, is frothing at the mouth and making wheezing noises. A tourniquet is around his upper arm and a needle and syringe (works) are on the floor.

Q. What should you do?

A. Because the casualty is unconscious you must check that he is breathing and has a pulse. Clear the airway if necessary and maintain it by placing the casualty in the recovery position. Get an ambulance to the scene as soon as possible and be prepared to resuscitate if necessary.

See Emergency Treatment, page 61

Note: Induced vomiting

Avoid making the casualty vomit as it may harm him further and is considered to be an ineffective remedy.

Comment

Your main consideration at any such incident must of course be your prime duty to protect life. However there are many other things for you to think about in these vital early minutes. To help you consider all the issues, we have constructed a simple check list to safeguard yourself, the casualty and any relevant evidence:

Check list for scene of suspected drugs overdose

▶ Call an ambulance.
▶ Don't waste time, assess the situation carefully.
▶ Get help – it's more important to help the casualty in the short term.
▶ If you cannot maintain an airway you will have to move the casualty.
▶ Resuscitate the casualty if necessary.
▶ Place in the recovery position.
▶ Look out for needle marks or puncture wounds and bleeding.
▶ Use a coat, rug or blanket on the floor to protect the casualty from the cold and minimise the effects of medical shock.
▶ Look at the total picture.
▶ Protect yourself from any kind of infection.
▶ Talk to the person at all times in a reassuring manner.
▶ Watch what you say – don't talk *about* the casualty as he may hear you.
▶ Gather evidence safely and be aware of the continuity chain *(see chapter 7)*.
▶ It is important that you speak with the ambulance crew and if necessary hand over any substances believed to be responsible for the overdose so that medical staff are able to determine the nature of the substance involved.

Note: Evidential considerations

Your duty to protect life may not sit comfortably with the continuity of evidence and, in the event of any offences being revealed, you may need to obtain statements from others involved in the handling of exhibits to prove the chain of recovery. Don't forget to note down the identity of any witnesses and obtain the names of the ambulance crew; this could turn into a major investigation, so avoid any embarrassment and cover all the basics.

The bottom line is

▶ get your priorities right (ie people come before evidence)
▶ treat the person with care
▶ look for danger
▶ protect yourself.

[3] OTHER ILLNESSES

Q. What if the illness is not a drugs overdose, but has some other cause?

A. In the scenario described earlier, the circumstances pointed to drug abuse. However it may be that the casualty is diabetic and has fallen ill.

Difficulties may exist, particularly if the casualty is unconscious or uncooperative, in establishing what has caused the illness. A check of any pockets or baggage in the possession of the person may provide evidence which will lead to an early diagnosis and swifter treatment for the person. An example of this would be a medical card which tells you that the person is on medication, or provides other medical details which may reveal a history of epilepsy or other illness.

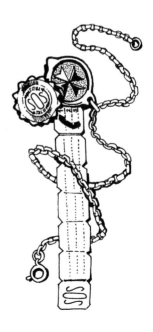

In addition to such items being found, a check of pockets etc may even result in medication being recovered from the casualty. This could give important pointers about the cause of the illness.

For example, 'Phenobarbitone' or 'Phenytoin' is taken for epilepsy or 'Glyceryl trinitrate' for angina. Other items which may help in discovering the cause of illness are medical warning items such as 'SOS Talisman' or 'Medical-Alert' and which may be worn as medallions, bracelets, lockets or other personal items such as key rings.

Inside these items you will usually find a piece of paper, folded in concertina fashion, giving details of the person, or relatives to be informed in an emergency and warnings in respect of the illness.

A telephone number for details about the casualty's medical history is often included to assist medical staff in diagnosing and treating the person.

Other items found while checking pockets of the casualty may immediately point to more common illnesses. For example inhalers, often referred to as 'puffers', are sometimes carried by asthmatics, indigestion tablets may suggest a stomach ulcer and insulin syringes or sugar lumps point to the casualty being diabetic.

All these things are indicators that could help in making sure the person receives appropriate treatment. These indicators may also be useful in identifying the person, to enable us to inform their relatives. Remember also to safeguard the casualty's property and avoid any subsequent complaints.

If you suspect drug abuse beware of needles and syringes which may expose you to the infections mentioned earlier in this chapter

APPENDIX

Emergency treatment checklist

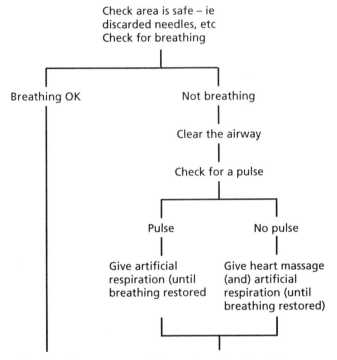

Check area is safe – ie discarded needles, etc
Check for breathing

Breathing OK

Not breathing

Clear the airway

Check for a pulse

Pulse

No pulse

Give artificial respiration (until breathing restored

Give heart massage (and) artificial respiration (until breathing restored)

Place in the recovery position and monitor breathing.
DO NOT LEAVE THE VICTIM.

CONCLUSION

The chapter was not written from a medical perspective, but rather from a common sense point of view aimed at providing good advice which has been gathered from many sources, such as:

- the Department of Health
- the Health Education Authority
- various drug advisory groups
- the St John Ambulance Voluntary Organisation
- the Institute for the Study of Drug Dependence

as well as personal advice from a number of practitioners involved in advising and training those who work with drug users.

We have attempted to collate and synthesise the information and package it in such a way as to promote 'best practice'.

We have also assumed that, like us, you will have received some basic first aid training and are able to respond to emergencies in a practical way.

We feel this chapter is essential in assisting you to fulfil the prime function of the police service, that of preserving life, and complements the remainder of the book which is directed towards our other functions of preventing and detecting crime and securing evidence.

Chapter 4

DRUGS STOP AND SEARCH

INTRODUCTION

Given the danger which substance abuse presents for the individual and society at large, it follows that there must be controls, and the first line of law enforcement is the 'Stop and Search Powers' exercised by the police, in relation to the possession of drugs. They are neatly contained within that key legislative instrument, the Misuse of Drugs Act 1971[1 see overleaf] which gives constables the power to search persons, vehicles or vessels for controlled drugs.

However, except in Scotland, the exercise of these powers is subject to further control by the Codes of Practice issued under the umbrella of the Police and Criminal Evidence Act 1984, in particular, Code A, which regulates 'the exercise by police officers of statutory powers of stop and search'.[2 see overleaf]

Code A emphasises that the power to stop and search must be 'used responsibly' and cautions officers that they may well be required to justify their use of such powers to senior officers and to a court. The watchwords for officers must be *objectivity*, in deciding upon the need for a search, and consideration and *courtesy*, when carrying it out.

This chapter combines the legislative directions and gives practical advice in relation to:

S

(1) **Q. Does the Misuse of Drugs Act 1971 apply to Scotland?**
     A. The short answer to this question is yes. It gives constables the power to search persons, vehicles or vessels for controlled drugs.

(2) **Q. Do the Codes of Practice referred to throughout this book apply to Scotland?**
     A. No. However, it would be helpful for a Scots police officer to read them and, where they do not conflict with the principles of Scots law and/or Force instructions, there would appear to be no reason why the officer could not use the advice given.

Scots law does not contain a comprehensive set of rules similar to the Codes of Practice created by the Police and Criminal Evidence Act 1984. This is because so much turns upon the exact circumstances of the case and it is from these that the court will decide whether or not the police exercised 'fairness to the accused'. Basically, all a Scots officer has to do in exercising 'fairness to the accused' is to use common sense and remember that anything obtained as a result of improper or illegitimate means can never be admitted in evidence.

[A] Search with consent

Q. Is it necessary to use the powers granted to police officers to stop and search people for drugs?

Code A
1D(b)

A. On the face of it the answer is no. Indeed Code A of the Codes of Practice, which governs drugs stop and searches, clearly advises that when no search power exists, officers can search anyone or anything with the appropriate consent. It also advises that the officer obtain full and informed consent, making it clear to the person that he need not consent and that if he does not consent, he will not be searched.

S

Q. Must Scots officers always use their powers under the Misuse of Drugs Act 1971 to stop and search a person for drugs?

A. It is strongly recommended that, whenever circumstances permit, an officer should use the powers granted under s 23 of the Misuse of Drugs Act 1971.

However, although not recommended, it may be possible under Scots common law, for an officer to search a person without warrant, if that person consents to being searched. In such cases, the officer must ensure that the consent by that person (and the search) is witnessed by a reliable witness.

Should officers use this practice, they must realise, that if drugs were found on the person who consented to be searched, the courts will scrutinise the police actions to ensure that 'fairness to the accused' was exercised. In particular, the courts will be anxious to ensure the officer did not act illegally, by searching a person in order to discover evidence to determine whether or not he should be apprehended.

▶

JUVENILES, MENTALLY HANDICAPPED, OR DISORDERED PERSONS

Code A 1E	The same code advises that juveniles, mentally handicapped, mentally disordered persons or those who appear unable to give informed consent should not be subjected to a voluntary search.

In practice, the operative words of advice are 'when no power exists', suggesting strongly that – if you have a power – use it, thereby avoiding any future arguments concerning the extent of any informed consent, or the degree of consent given, or the point at which consent was withdrawn. This does not mean that you cannot enlist the voluntary co-operation of the person concerned to assist you to complete the search quickly and professionally. Some officers use consent rather than co-operation because it saves paperwork, but it does expose the officer and the evidence to danger. What is more, Forces usually require search records to be completed even in cases of consent, so check your force policy. Consent searches should be a last resort, not an initial action.

S ► This principle was made clear by Lord Robertson in the case of *Jackson v Stevenson 34 SLR 430*, when he stated:

> 'I know of no authority for ascribing to constables the right to make... tentative searches,... they seem contrary to constitutional principle. If the constable requires to make such a search, it can only be because without it he is not justified in apprehending and, without warrant, to search a person not liable to apprehension seems palpably illegal.'

[B] Stop and search powers

This section covers stop and search powers without arrest, in relation to persons, vehicles and vessels.

Q. What are the powers granted to police officers?
A. Section 23(2) of the Misuse of Drugs Act 1971 gives constables three related powers:

> ▶ to search people (allowing that person to be detained, **not arrested**, long enough to carry out the search)
> ▶ to search any vehicle or vessel (giving the officer the power to require the person in control to stop it)
> ▶ to seize and detain evidence of any offence under the Misuse of Drug Act which is found in the course of the search

provided that the constable has 'reasonable grounds to suspect' that any person is in possession of a 'controlled drug' and in the case of a vehicle or vessel, that the officer 'suspects' that the drugs may be found in it. [4]

S

[4] In this section a Scots officer is granted the same powers of stop and search as detailed in s 23 of the Misuse of Drugs Act 1971.

Note

When detaining a person under the provisions of s 23 of the Misuse of Drugs Act 1971, avoid the use of the word 'arrest' when informing the suspect of your powers. This stems from the case of *Wither v Reid* 1979, SLT 192, in which an officer informed a suspect that she was under arrest when dealing with her under s 23(2)(a) of the Act. The court held that the arrest was unlawful, as s 23(2)(a) only gave the police power to detain a person for the purpose of a drug search.

Comment

Provided it is used correctly in accordance with PACE, this power is an excellent tool when investigating drug offences. Abusers are often confident individuals who will 'score' their drugs from the home of suppliers or licensed premises and then walk home, take a taxi or drive a vehicle to a place where they will either use the substance or further distribute it.

S

Q. If a person has been detained for the purposes of a search under s 23 of the Misuse of Drugs Act 1971, is there any prohibition on continuing his detention under the provisions of s 2(1) of the Criminal Justice (Scotland) Act 1980 (ie the six-hour period of detention permitted, when a person is reasonably suspected of having committed an offence punishable by imprisonment), once the reason for the original detention has been satisfied?

A. The answer to this question is a qualified yes, as s 2(3A) of the Criminal Justice (Scotland) Act 1980 states: 'Where a person has previously been detained in pursuance of any enactment or subordinate instrument, he may not be detained under s 2(1) of this Act, on the same grounds or on grounds arising from the same circumstances which led to his earlier detention.

[5] With regard to the offence of obstruction under s 23(4) of the Misuse of Drugs Act 1971, a Scots officer derives his power of arrest from s 24 of the Act which provides:

'A constable may arrest without warrant a person who has committed, or whom the constable, with reasonable cause, suspects to have committed, an offence under the Misuse of Drugs Act 1971 if:

Note: Obstruction/arrest [5]

Section 23(4) of the Misuse of Drugs Act 1971 also created the offence of obstruction which is committed by any person who intentionally obstructs a constable exercising the powers of stop and search described above. The power of arrest being that granted under s 25 of PACE, ie the general arrest conditions.

S ▶

(a) he, with reasonable cause, believes that that person will abscond unless arrested; or

(b) the name and address of that person are unknown to, and cannot be ascertained by, him, or

(c) he is not satisfied that a name and address furnished by that person as his name and address are true.'

The power of arrest granted under s 24 of the Act is limited by the conditions laid down in paragraphs (a)-(c) above. However, if the conditions contained in (a)-(c) are not present to justify an arrest under the Act, you may still arrest an accused using your common law powers (see s 3 of the *Scottish Criminal Law* manual).

Note

In the case of *Carmichael v Brannan* 1985 SCCR 234, where it was held that 'obstructs' in s 23(4)(a) of the Act, was not limited to physical obstruction, but covered any act done with intent to hinder officers in the discharge of their duties.

Q. Is it possible to charge a person with obstruction under s 41 of the Police (Scotland) Act 1967 instead of obstruction under s 23(4) of the Misuse of Drugs Act 1971?

A. Yes, provided the provisions contained in s 41 of the Police (Scotland) Act 1967 have been contravened by the accused.

▶

Q. What does 'reasonable grounds to suspect' mean?

A. This is very much a matter for the individual officer. Remember that you may have to explain to a senior officer or a court just what your grounds were. Whether the reasonable grounds for suspicion exist will depend on the circumstances in each case, but there must be some objective basis for it. In other words you, as the officer involved, would require more than a mere hunch before you could lawfully detain a person for the stop and search procedure to be carried out.

S   Under Scots law, the question of whether an officer had 'reasonable grounds to suspect' within the context of s 23 of the Misuse of Drugs Act 1971, is a question of law for the judge in any trial involving the use of this power. Basically this involves the judge considering the fundamental principle of 'fairness to the accused', within the circumstances of the case under review.

| Code A 1.7 | Code A gives some guidance about what is meant by 'reasonable suspicion', particularly by telling us what is not reasonable. It stresses the following points: |

❭ not personal factors such as:
  • race/colour
  • age
  • hairstyle
  • manner of dress
  • appearance
  (and, of course, there are many more)
❭ not previous convictions
❭ no stereotypes of persons or groups thought more likely to commit such offences

none of which either alone or in combination with each other can amount to 'reasonable suspicion'.

| Code A p 1.7A | Code A also states that persons innocently in possession of items for which a constable is empowered to search, in this case 'controlled drugs' may, provided that there is reasonable suspicion, be subject to a stop and search, even though there is no power to arrest. It goes on to stress the importance of enlisting a persons' co-operation to produce the article, before resorting to force as a last resort. |

> ### Example
> You are very much aware that a particular individual living on your beat has four convictions for unlawful possession of cannabis. This doesn't surprise you because of the person's appearance and you've always thought that he looks the type. Based on these grounds you decide to try and make it five convictions. So you lie in wait until the person comes out of his house where you detain him and carry out a search for drugs.

The Police and Criminal Evidence Act tells you that under these circumstances there were no reasonable grounds to suspect possession of drugs and therefore the carrying out of the stop and search procedure would be unlawful. A decided case may assist you to decide what is or is not reasonable suspicion:

Note: *Tomlinson v DPP*

In the case of *Tomlinson v DPP*: Legal Action May, 1992, p 21, two plain clothes police officers on patrol in an area 'renowned for drugs' watched a man for 15 minutes. They saw him walking about aimlessly, stopping and looking about him. He did not stop or talk to anyone. He was spoken to by the officers and reacted in a hostile way. The officers identified themselves and told him that they suspected him of being in possession of a controlled drug and wished to search him. Before he could be searched, a struggle took place and the man was charged with and convicted of assaulting a constable acting in the execution of her duty. He appealed to the Divisional Court of the Queens Bench Division which found that, although there was no doubt that the officers genuinely suspected that the defendant was in possession of drugs, there were no reasonable grounds for this belief. The defendant's behaviour was not indicative of any offence and could be consistent with many explanations. The court upheld the appeal.

Comment

If you receive information from a reliable source that a person is in possession of a controlled drug then this would provide a concrete basis for carrying out the search because your suspicion would be reasonable. Similarly your attention may be drawn to a person whose behaviour appears strange and – after speaking with them and satisfying yourself that the person is not drunk or ill – you may feel you have reasonable grounds to carry out a search to establish the presence of drugs because the person's condition leads you to suspect that he may be in possession of a substance.

Equally the person detained may give a satisfactory explanation for his actions and although you have detained him for a search you now feel it is unnecessary to carry it out. If you make this decision PACE says the persons' detention will not be unlawful.

Q. How do I go about searching a person?

A. Except in Scotland, the search itself is controlled or guided by Code A of PACE. It breaks the process down into easy stages, which we will cover in turn, giving practical advice on 'best practice'.

ACTION BEFORE THE SEARCH

CODE A
2.1 2.2
2A

The Code of Practice makes three key points concerning action before a search.

▶ The officer must have reasonable suspicion before beginning the process and there is no power to detain a person in order to develop that suspicion by questioning him.

▶ Having decided that there is reasonable suspicion, the officer may decide to question the person concerned about the facts which gave rise to the suspicion, thereby possibly eliminating the need for a search, either because the substance has been produced or the officer decides that there are no grounds for the search and releases the individual.

▶ Such preliminary questioning may confirm or eliminate the need for the search, but cannot be used retrospectively as grounds for the search.

Comment

The key point here is the fact that the power of detention may be used only for the search itself and/or any preliminary questions concerning it. It cannot be used to create or 'firm up' reasonable suspicion prior to a search.

In practice, having decided to stop and search a person for drugs, watch carefully as you approach. The person may well try to swallow or throw away the drugs, or even reveal where they are likely to be hidden by 'checking' involuntarily with their hands.

ACTION ON CARRYING OUT THE SEARCH

Once again the Code of Practice requires that certain information must be given to the detained person, including the following:

> ❱ your name
> ❱ the object of the search
> ❱ your grounds/authorisation for undertaking the search.

Also:

> ❱ you must show your warrant card if not in uniform
> ❱ inform the person to be searched that he is entitled to a copy of the 'record of search' at any time within the next 12 months
> ❱ *and* (if the person wants a copy) *either*
> – give him a copy on the spot; *or*
> – tell him at which police station he can apply for one.

Comment

The Code of Practice uses the wording 'reasonable steps', when discussing the verbal information to be given in relation to a search, and the wording 'practicable', when discussing the provision of the written search record.

In other words it does accept the real possibility that circumstances like a violent detainee, or a heavy downpour of rain may interfere with the process.

However the dangers of non-compliance are aptly demonstrated through a decided case which was heard at Acton Crown Court.

Note: *R v Fennelley*

In the case of *R v Fennelley* [1989] CrimLR 142, a person was charged with possession of Heroin with intent to supply. The police stopped and searched the defendant in the street believing that he was dealing in drugs, but no drugs were found until later when he was strip searched at the police station, and two packets of heroin were found. The prosecution could not prove that he had been told why he had been stopped, searched and arrested. The court decided that, as he might have provided an explanation had he been informed of the reasons for being stopped, it was unfair to admit the evidence obtained in this way. The evidence of the stop and search and of the finding of two packets was excluded under s 78 of PACE.

Note: Searches of deaf or foreign persons

Where there is any doubt that the person searched does not understand what is said, or does not appear to speak English, the officer must – here are those words again – take reasonable steps to bring both the verbal and written information concerning the search to his or her notice. The Code also suggests that, in cases where a person who may be deaf or who cannot understand English is with someone, that person may be co-opted to help to provide the necessary information.

Having made the decision to search the person for drugs you will be asking yourself questions like:

> ▶ How far am I going to search?
> ▶ Where shall I conduct the search?

There are many considerations, not least of which is the fact that drugs can easily be concealed about the body and in the lining of clothes etc. Your level of suspicion will determine how far you will search. The Codes of Practice require you to consider:

Code A 3.1 to 3.5 3A & 3B

(i) Dignity
Every effort must be made to minimise the embarrassment experienced by the person being searched

(ii) Co-operation
Seek the co-operation (not the consent) of the person to be searched, even if he initially objected to the search. Force may only be used as a last resort, even then only reasonable force may be used to conduct a search or to detain a person for such a search.

(iii) Time factors
The length of time for which a person may be detained will depend on the circumstances, but the Codes of Practice recognise that in cases involving small articles such as drugs, which might be concealed anywhere on the person, a more extensive search may be necessary.

(iv) Depth of search
Searches in public must be restricted to superficial examination of outer clothing and there is no power to require a person to remove any clothing in public (which includes an empty street) other than an outer coat, jacket or gloves.

However, you may *ask* a person to remove appropriate items of clothing in public, but you cannot require it of him.

(v) Who can search

If the search involves the removal of more than an outer coat, jacket, gloves, headgear or footwear it may only be made by an officer of the same sex as the person searched and may not be made in the presence of anyone of the opposite sex unless the person being searched specifically requests it.

(vi) Location of search

The search must be conducted at or near the place where the person was first detained. Obviously there are times when you will need to conduct a thorough search of a person and of course this will need to be done in private, say in a police van or at a nearby police station.

SEARCH AT THE POLICE STATION

There appears to be some controversy about where a search under the Misuse of Drugs Act 1971 and governed by the Codes of Practice can take place. Some supervisory officers argue that on the basis of *Arnold v Kingston-upon Hull Chief Constable* [1969] or *Dongeni v Ward* [1969] 1 WLR 1502, that a search cannot take place at a police station unless it is within either one and a half miles, or 160 yards. However, others argue that, on the basis of *Farrow v Tunnicliffe* [1976] Crim LR 126 DC (in which, following a superficial search, the officers concerned removed two suspects some distance to a police station) an officer can require a person detained for a stop and search to go to a police station. Code A 3.5, seems to endorse this point saying that a more extensive search must not be done in public view, giving examples of a police van or nearby police station as suitable alternatives.

These decided cases also have an effect when you get to the police station. Some custody officers will not allow drugs searches to be carried out in the custody suite; others will allow them to be carried out but will not open a custody record, arguing quite properly that the person is not under arrest and is therefore not a PACE prisoner. Others will record the search on a custody record as a means of good practice, though obviously the person being searched will not be given any rights or entitlements under

PACE. Finally some custody officers will insist that the person be formally arrested on suspicion of possessing a Class A or Class B controlled drug (ie an arrestable offence under s 24 PACE 1984) and processed as a PACE prisoner.

On the face of it, it is all very confusing, but don't be put off. Practically, on the street, if you can conduct a search on the spot do so. If you can't, consider nearby premises or, failing that, use a police van. If you need to conduct a thorough search go to the nearest police station. There is little doubt that the best place for a full search is probably a police station, which is private, secure, well-lit and filled with a cornucopia of evidence bags, well trained staff, computer checks, and good advice. What is more the hard floors and lack of furnishings make it easy to spot anything discarded by a detained person, and the initial processing will probably be captured on the custody suite video.

The bottom line is be aware of your Force policy on where drugs searches can be done, discuss it with your supervisor, or better still your local custody officer – that way you will not fall foul of the legislation. For the record we accept *Farrow v Tunnicliffe* as the key decided case and argue that a record of the search can be useful when made on on a custody record, though we accept that the person is not a PACE prisoner.

ACTION AFTER THE SEARCH IS CARRIED OUT

| CODE A |
| 4.1 TO |
| 4.5 4A |

These actions concern the search record which must be completed as soon as practicable – normally on the spot – by the officer carrying out the search, unless it is not practicable to do so.

The Codes of Practice once again stipulate a series of rules which must be followed, these include:

▶ recording the search on the proper national form;
▶ seeking to include the name, address and date of birth of the person searched **(though people are under no obligation to give such details and there is no power to compel them to do so)**
▶ including the following details:

- the name of the person searched (or if the name is not given, the description)
- the person's ethnic origin
- the object of the search
- the grounds for making it, briefly detailing the reason(s) for the suspicion
- the date and time of the search
- the place of the search
- the result
- the identity of the officer who conducted the search (if more than one officer is involved this must include all their identities).

Comment

In practical terms, having decided on a stop and search, tell the person who you are and, if in plain clothes, produce your warrant card. If you can take hold of the person's hands to prevent them disposing of anything, do so. Similarly watch their mouth when they speak to see if anything is concealed there. Tell the suspect in clear simple language why you want to search, what you are looking for and where you are going to carry out the search.

Make a systematic search of the person's clothing and if necessary remove him to some place away from public view, ie nearby premises, a police van or even the nearest police station. Keep the person's hands in view at all times and, if you transport him anywhere, get him to keep his hands in view and search any vehicle used as transport. When you get to the place of search remove and examine each item of clothing and personal property closely, checking ties, belts, shoes, socks and the seams and padding in clothing.

Remember the dignity of the person and seek co-operation in the search rather than moving his limbs etc, and **remember to follow the rules concerning strip searches**, especially in relation to allowing the person to retain some item of clothing at all times, ie allow him to put a shirt back on before asking him to remove his underpants.

Remember too, that drug abusers can be infected with some highly contagious diseases so it is best if you ask if he has anything in his possession which is liable to injure you, before carrying out the search, ie a syringe. Wear disposable gloves and cover up any open cuts, etc.

Most importantly of all, talk to the person politely, explaining what you are doing, why you are doing it and what you want them to do. It is amazing what courtesy can do to improve the relationship between the searcher and the searched.

VEHICLE SEARCHES

Q. How do I go about searching a vehicle?

A. Remember the power to search vehicles and vessels is contained within s 23(2) of the Misuse of Drugs Act 1971 and is governed by the Codes of Practice.

Here are the key points:

Misuse of Drugs

Only those vehicles or vessels in which a constable suspects that a controlled drug is to be found may be stopped or detained (given that the officer must have reasonable grounds to suspect that a person is in possession of a controlled drug).

| Code A 2.4 | The officer must take reasonable steps to tell the person in charge of the vehicle his or her name (and if in plain clothes produce a warrant card), state the object of the search and the grounds/authorisation for it. |

| Code A 3.2 - 3.4 | Force may only be used as a last resort to detain a vehicle or vessel for a search. |

The time during which the vehicle (vessel) is detained must be reasonable given the circumstances and must not extend beyond the time taken for the search.

The search must be conducted near to where the vehicle was detained.

| CODE A 4.1 - 4.3 and 4.5 | After completing the search, the officer must, as soon as practicable, make a record of the search on the appropriate form (unless it is not practicable to do so). The record must include: |

▶ a description of the vehicle, indicating its registration number (providing it has one)
▶ the object of the search
▶ the grounds for making it
▶ the date and time of the search
▶ the place it was made
▶ the results
▶ any damage caused
▶ the identity of those involved in the search.

When the officer makes such a record, the owner of the vehicle or vessel, or person in charge of it, must be told of their entitlement to a copy, and the fact that this lasts for a year. If they require a copy they should either be given one on the spot or told which police station to apply to.

| Code A 2.7 | **Persons in charge who are foreign, deaf, etc** |

Similar provisions to those relating to the searching of *persons* who appear not to understand, are foreign or deaf, apply to person in charge of a *vehicle* to be searched.

Code A 4.6

One record for two searches

Although a search record is required for every search of a person or vehicle for drugs, when a person is present in a vehicle and both are searched only one record need be made.

Code A 4.8 - 4.10

Unattended vehicles

Sometimes it may be necessary to search an unattended vehicle for drugs, eg the owner having been arrested for possession of a controlled drug. In which case:

▶ If a search of the interior or exterior is carried out a notice must be left in or on the vehicle.
▶ The notice should include the name of the police station to which the officer concerned is attached and state where a copy of the record of the search can be obtained and where any application for compensation should be made.
▶ The vehicle must (if practicable) be left secure.

Vehicles are important when considering importation offences or large scale drug supplying; or even simple possession.

The number of hiding places in vehicles seem endless and that is why great care must be taken when searching. Where vehicles are used in street level drug abuse the drugs are more likely to be found in places that are easily accessible and a search may well be restricted to the following areas:

▶ glove compartments
▶ visors
▶ door panels
▶ behind ash trays
▶ beneath carpets
▶ under the spare wheel.

▶ A check should also be made of roof linings for signs or openings where a substance could be concealed.

[C] Search upon arrest

Q. What power do I have to search a person after arresting them for an offence? (6 see overleaf)

A. The power to search is conferred by s 32 PACE, provided that the arrest takes place away from the police station. The key power in relation to drugs is in fact conferred by subs (2) of the section giving the officer the power to search for anything which may be evidence of an offence. Thus although it is likely that the person will have been arrested for possession, either by virtue of it being an arrestable offence (s 24 PACE for possession of a Class A or B controlled drug), or under the general arrest conditions (s 25 PACE), an officer can search for drugs following any arrest providing that the officer has a 'reasonable belief' that the person may have concealed a controlled substance, or any other evidence in relation to drugs offences such as drugs paraphernalia, client lists, etc. (Do not forget the need to notionally arrest for these additional offences.)

The search is limited in its extent to that reasonably required to discover the evidence sought and, like a stop and search, is restricted to the removal in public of only the outer coat, jacket and gloves.

The officer has the power to seize and retain any evidence of an offence or anything obtained in consequence of the commission of an offence (except for items of legal privilege) (s 32(9)).

Comment

In practice such searches are generally superficial, given that it is likely that the custody officer will authorise a more extensive search when the suspect is delivered to the police station. However the fact that the person is a prisoner should not detract from considering his dignity, or seeking his co-operation. Similarly be aware of the dangers from a needle stick injury or the possibility that the suspect will dispose of, secrete or conceal any evidence of drugs. As always the watchword is vigilance.

Q. What are the relevant powers of arrest? [7 see overleaf]

A. To assist officers in determining their arrest powers we have linked the main offences in relation to drugs together with their power of arrest.

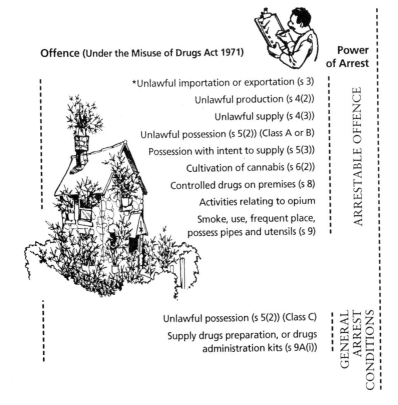

Offence (Under the Misuse of Drugs Act 1971)   **Power of Arrest**

*Unlawful importation or exportation (s 3)

Unlawful production (s 4(2))

Unlawful supply (s 4(3))

Unlawful possession (s 5(2)) (Class A or B)

Possession with intent to supply (s 5(3))

Cultivation of cannabis (s 6(2))

Controlled drugs on premises (s 8)

Activities relating to opium

Smoke, use, frequent place, possess pipes and utensils (s 9)

ARRESTABLE OFFENCE

Unlawful possession (s 5(2)) (Class C)

Supply drugs preparation, or drugs administration kits (s 9A(i))

GENERAL ARREST CONDITIONS

Note

Section 3 of the Misuse of Drugs Act 1971 provides for unlawful importation/exportation under the Customs Management Act 1979.

S

(6) ▶ Under the common law, the police in Scotland are empowered to search without warrant any person who has been apprehended, to find any of the articles which may have assisted him in, or are the products of, the crime or offence which he may have committed.

▶ This power of search may, if circumstances so dictate, be exercised on the spot.

▶ The *Scottish Criminal Law* manual advises police officers to make a thorough search of every person detained in custody. This should be done with tact, with the prisoner being informed that the search is being carried out in accordance with police procedure.

▶ With regard to the actual form the search should take, Scots officers should consult their own *Force Procedure* manuals.

(7) The term 'arrestable offence' is not used in Scots law. Scottish officers should refer to s 24 of the Misuse of Drugs Act 1971 (above) for their powers of arrest.

In addition, they may be able to use their more liberal common law powers of arrest, if the circumstances allow

[D] Seizure

So far we have discussed the powers of stop and search with and without consent and the authority we have to seize items of evidential value. It is important that the evidence obtained is dealt with properly.

SEIZURE, SUCCESS AND SAFETY

A good start would be to make sure the initial recovery is handled correctly and that serious consideration is given to safeguarding yourself against unnecessary allegations. Another important factor is to be mindful of the continuity chain in order to prove that the substance recovered from the suspect is in fact the substance finally identified and analysed for evidential purposes.

There are a number of different ways to package drugs for sending to the forensic science laboratories and procedures differ from force to force, and even from country to country. [8]

Which ever system of packaging is used the importance of dealing properly with the initial recovery cannot be over-emphasised.

S
[8] All Scottish officers should know the general advice contained in the *Scottish Criminal Law* manual, namely that when they seize an item which has possible evidential value in a case it becomes a 'production'.

Thereafter, at the earliest possible moment, the item (apart from documents) should have attached to it a sealed label signed and dated by each witness who is to testify to it as a production, including the officer who took possession of it. A documentary production should be signed or initialled and dated by the witnesses and police officers concerned. Only when it is not convenient to mark a document, may a sealed label be attached.

The advice on how to deal with seizure and storage of productions in drug cases will be contained in your *Force Procedure* manuals and you should consult these for yourself as there may be variations from one force to another

Let us consider the straightforward street recovery involving a piece of cannabis from a stop and search. If you are in possession of a Tamper Evident Bag at all times and you are able to enclose the cannabis and seal it securely in accordance with your guidelines then do so. Do not simply place the cannabis in your pocket for production to the custody officer later, as this could present trouble for you should allegations about your handling of the substance be made.

Imagine how you would feel if, when you produce the cannabis during interview, the suspect suggests that the recovery is now smaller than when seized and accuses you of stealing it. This risk is unnecessary. If you are unable to carry Tamper Evident Bags on patrol, then consider keeping a manilla envelope handy, preferably of the window type.

You can then place your recovery in the envelope, seal it in the presence of the suspect and request that he sign across the seal at the time of recovery. If the suspect refuses you can then record the refusal over the seal.

If the envelope is the window type, the custody officer will be able to see the substance without having to open the envelope which should only be opened during interview for re-packaging in accordance with your force guidelines.

During interview reference can be made to the initial recovery, how it was made, and the fact that the seal of the envelope containing the substance remains unbroken and either bears the suspect's signature to confirm this, or the recorded refusal.

When re-packaging for laboratory purposes it is vital that this envelope is also packaged with the substance to prove continuity. You may feel this is adding to your workload but think about the possibility of unnecessary complaints.

Chapter 5

SEARCHING PREMISES

INTRODUCTION

The searching of premises must be carried out professionally. To do otherwise risks your evidence, your reputation, and even your health. As a constable, or supervisor, it is essential that you negotiate your route through the maze of overlapping, sometimes confusing powers of entry, search and seizure and choose the right power for the right premises for the right reason. This chapter is divided into eight sections designed to lead you systematically through these powers and provide practical tips and checklists to use alongside them, to help you get it right.

The searches are as follows:

S

Because PACE does not apply in Scotland, the chapter has a limited relevance to officers working there. For that reason we would direct your attention to particular sections of this chapter, as detailed below:

[A] Searches Without Warrant see footnote (9)

[B] Searches Under Warrant see footnotes (10) and (11)

[C] [F]   Have little or no relevance to Scotland as Scottish officers will be required to follow the guidance contained in their own force procedures.

[G] 'Practical tips' is highly relevant to all officers conducting or supervising drugs searches in premises.

[H] Other considerations relating to children and informants is also relevant.

[A] Search without Warrant

[1] ENTRY AND SEARCH FOR THE PURPOSE OF ARREST

Q. What power do I have to enter premises, search them and ultimately arrest the person sought, without a warrant?

| PACE A s17 | A. The answer is s 17 PACE, providing of course the offence concerned is an 'arrestable offence' as defined by s 24 PACE. |

Listed below are the main drug offences which are 'arrestable' by reason of their possible prison sentence, ie exceeding five years.

- ▶ Unlawful importation – exportation.
- ▶ Unlawful production.
- ▶ Cultivation of cannabis.
- ▶ Unlawful supply.
- ▶ Occupying – managing premises.
- ▶ Opium-related offences ie these detailed in s 9 Misuse of Drugs Act 1971.
- ▶ Unlawful possession with intent to supply.
- ▶ Unlawful possession of class A and B controlled drugs.

S [9] Searches without warrant, ss 17, 18, 19 and 32 PACE, do not apply to Scotland.

The police in Scotland have no general power by virtue of their office to enter private premises without warrant in order to search for evidence. However, in the case of *HM Advocate v McGuigan* 1936 SLT, the High Court of Justiciary held that, where the matter is one of urgency, the police may be entitled to search premises without a warrant and/or the permission of the owner or occupants.

Whether or not a search without warrant, in cases of urgency, is lawful, and any evidence obtained is admissible, is a question of circumstances and in each case the court will balance the public interest against the interest of the accused in reaching a decision.

▶

Let us look at the key proviso of s 17, PACE, which empowers a constable to enter (using reasonable force when necessary) and search any premises to arrest a person for an arrestable offence. It states that such power is only exercisable if you, the constable, have reasonable grounds for believing that the person you seek to arrest is on the premises. An example might help to explain this proviso:

S ▶ The basic criteria for the Scottish officer is that – where he has arrested a person on a grave charge – a search without warrant of his home etc, would be justified if the ends of justice are likely to be defeated by the delay necessary in obtaining a search warrant.

On the other hand, where the arrest concerns a minor charge or where urgency is not of prime consideration, a search without warrant would not be justified.

It is also possible to search premises, receptacles etc, without warrant when the police obtain the consent of the individual(s) concerned. In such cases, care must be taken to ensure that such consent is obtained in the presence of a reliable witness and, whenever practicable, the person giving the consent should be present during the search.

Example

You are on duty when you receive reliable information from a tried and tested source to the effect that Page has broken into a doctor's motor car and stolen his medical bag which contains a quantity of drugs and prescription pads. You are told that Page is at his bed-sit now and is ringing round people to off-load the prescriptions.

You have confirmed the information is accurate and you decide to arrest Page.

Look now at the relevant part of s 17, PACE. You will see that this power covers these circumstances well, as you would have reasonable grounds for believing that Page is on the premises.

PAGE IS
IN THE
BUILDING

Another example might clarify things further:

Example

If you knew that Page was at Turner's home discussing the events of the coming weekend and their intention to attend a 'rave' in Manchester you would be wrong to enter Page's bed-sit to have a look around and wait until he arrived home.

But you could of course exercise your s 17 power at Turner's home and arrest Page there.

Q. What premises can I enter?

PACE
s17

A. 'Premises' should be given its widest meaning and includes everything from off-shore installations to moveable structures like 'Portacabins', even tents. There are, however, some restrictions relating to 'communal premises'. Again an example might help:

Example

Contrast Turner's house with Page's bed-sit, one of several flats within a large Victorian house, in which tenants share communal facilities such as a bathroom, kitchen and TV room.

Let's look again at s 17(2(6)) PACE in relation to premises, which states that, where premises are made up of two or more separate dwellings, your powers of entry and search are limited to:

▶ any dwelling, such as a flat or bed-sit, where you, the constable, have reasonable grounds for believing that the person you are seeking to arrest is present

and

▶ any part of the premises which the various occupiers of the premises use in common, such as communal bathrooms, kitchens, TV room, lounge and the like.

Remember also that you can only search to the extent necessary to find the person you are seeking. In other words you can only look for Page in spaces big enough for him to hide, not drawers or kitchen cabinets, and you must stop searching the moment that he is found.

PACE s19 CODE B 6.1	Being lawfully on premises, you can seize anything that you have reasonable grounds for believing to be:

▶ obtained in consequence of the commission of an offence;

and/or

▶ evidence of any offence
to prevent such items being concealed, lost, damaged, altered or destroyed.

Remember too that any such search is subject to the provisions of Code B of the Codes of Practice, setting out the 'general conditions' for the searching of premises. It requires such things as the provision of a 'Notice of Powers and Rights' to the occupier etc.

Comment

The important thing to remember is that the objective of the entry and search is to arrest a suspect not seek evidence.

Therefore though you may chance upon items 'obtained in consequence of the commission of an offence'; 'evidence of the offence you are investigating'; and 'evidence of any offence'; you cannot actively search for such items. Most importantly, you must stop searching when you have found and arrested the suspect. If you then need to search for evidence etc, you must use s 18 or 32 of PACE, obtain a search warrant, or obtain consent. If you want to search Page himself you could use your s 32 powers *(see Chapter 4).*

[2] ENTRY FOR THE PURPOSE OF SEARCHING FOR EVIDENCE

Q. What powers do I have to enter premises to search for and seize evidence?

A. There are two relevant sections of PACE which give you the power of entry and search for evidence and one which gives you the power to seize it:

> ◗ section 32(2(b)) PACE (power of entry and search) plus s 19 PACE (power of seizure), or
> ◗ section 18 PACE (power of entry, search and seizure).

The former (s 32) relates to searching premises following an arrest for any offence. The latter (s 18) relates to searching premises following an arrest for an arrestable offence (s 24, PACE). We will deal with each in turn:

PACE s32

This section confers the power to enter and search premises following any arrest. Under this power, after arresting a person for any offence, a constable can enter and search either:

◗ the premises in which the person was arrested

or

◗ the premises the arrested person left immediately before being arrested

provided

◗ that you, the constable, have reasonable grounds for believing that you will find evidence on the premises, relating to the offence for which the person was arrested

and

◗ that you limit the extent of your search to that reasonably required to find the evidence in question.

Comment

There are a number of key terms within this section which are worthy of explanation. We shall deal with each in turn;

'Premises in which the person was arrested or left immediately before being arrested'

To begin with the person must be arrested at a place other than at a police station, otherwise s 32 does not apply. What is more, the premises must be those in which the person was arrested, or the last premises he left immediately before being arrested.

Like s 17 PACE, the term 'premises' extends to the communal areas of those premises 'consisting of two or more dwellings'. In our earlier example involving Page, you would be able to search Page's bed-sit, and any communal areas in Page's, building, such as a bathroom, kitchen or lounge and if he had come straight from Turner's house, you would be able to search Turner's house also.

'Immediately'

This word can also present problems, being defined not in terms of miles/metres, or hours/minutes, but rather in terms of proximity of both geography and time, being the last premises the person left before being arrested.

Example

Thus, if Page had escaped from his window and been arrested in the street, his home would be the last premises he left and not Turner's house, which therefore could not be searched under this power.

'Extent'

There are also limitations relating to the extent of the search, restricting it to a search for evidence of the offence for which the arrest took place. Once again an example might help:

Example

In addition to searching for the prescription pads stolen by Page you could surely search for:

   ❱ any drugs obtained via the prescriptions;
   ❱ the doctor's bag and its contents;
   ❱ the keys or any other implement used to gain entry to the doctor's car.

Q. Given that s 32 PACE is only a power to enter and search for evidence, how can I seize and retain the evidence I may find?
A. Having entered any premises lawfully you may seize anything (except items of legal privilege) found on those premises.

PACE
s19

This is providing the constable has reasonable grounds for believing that the seizure was necessary to prevent:

   ❱ an item obtained in consequence of the commission of an offence, being – concealed, lost, altered, damaged or destroyed
   ❱ evidence of an offence currently being investigated or any other offence, being concealed, lost, altered or destroyed
   ❱ information contained in a computer which is evidence of an offence being investigated or any other offence, being concealed, lost, tampered with or destroyed.

Comment

Although you are restricted in the extent of your search under
s 32 PACE to that necessary to find the evidence for the offence
for which the person was arrested, s 19 PACE allows you not
only to seize the evidence which you have sought but, in addition, evidence of any other offences and any items obtained as a
result of the commission of any offence. In other words you cannot search for such extra items which you suspect may be on the
premises concerned, but you may seize any such items you come
across in the course of your 's 32' search. Returning to our
example:

Example

You could seize the stolen prescription pads, and any money made from
selling the prescription forms or any
drugs obtained by tendering the
stolen prescriptions; and any other
illegal drugs; and any computer
records of persons supplied with prescription forms or drugs: This could
even include other items not connected with drugs, such as a stolen video
or an illegal firearm.

Note: Notional arrests

Remember that if you seize evidence of other offences you will surely be required to make additional notional arrests under s 31 PACE.

| PACE s18 |

Power to enter and search premises and seize evidence following an arrest for an arrestable offence. Under this power, after arresting a person for an arrestable offence, a constable can enter (using reasonable force if necessary) and search either:

❯ premises occupied by the arrested person; or
❯ premises controlled by the arrested person.

If you, the constable, have reasonable grounds for suspecting that on the premises you will find evidence, of either

❯ that arrestable offence; or
❯ some other arrestable offence connected/similar to that offence

you may seize and retain anything for which were searching under this section of PACE.

Note: Limit of the search

As under s 32 PACE *(see page 96)*, the extent of the search is limited to that reasonably required to discover such evidence.

Comment

Once again a dip into our continuing Page saga may help to clarify your understanding of what is meant by 'occupied' or controlled:

Example

Let us suppose that Page escaped, but a day or two later gave himself up at a police station. Unlike s 32, under s 18 PACE the place of arrest is immaterial, it is the power of arrest which counts. Thus you could use all the powers of entry, search and seizure under s 18.

Later, during an interview, Page mentions the fact that while 'on the run' he had stayed at his favourite uncle's house. From remarks in his interview, you have reasonable grounds for believing that Page has secreted the missing prescription pads at his uncle's house. Page has told you that he occasionally spends an odd night at Uncle Bryan's, rather than return home. Unfortunately Page neither occupies or controls 'Uncle Bryan's' premises, making the fact of his 'last premises' before arrest a vital question.

Unfortunately it transpires that Page had called at the fish shop on his way to the police station, effectively rendering 'Uncle Bryan's' PACE-proof, unless there were grounds to arrest him for an arrestable offence.

Fortunately, Uncle Bryan is an honest man and allows you to search his premises with his full consent. You find a few prescription forms, but the bulk remain missing. Uncle Bryan tells you that his nephew and Turner presently lease a garage near to Turner's house in which things are kept out of sight. Since it is controlled by Page you are now able to enter it (by force if necessary) and seize the remainder of the prescription pads hidden there.

Note: Authorising the search

PACE s18

A search under s 18 PACE must be authorised in writing by an inspector (normally on the Notice of Powers and Rights). However, it is possible to make such a search after arresting a person for an arrestable offence but before taking him to the police station, without an inspector's authorisation – if the presence of the person at a place other than a police station is necessary for the effective investigation of the offence. In such a case the officer must inform an inspector as soon as practicable.

Note: Recording the search

PACE s18

The officer informed of the search, or authorising it, must record the grounds for the search

and

the 'nature of the evidence' sought.

Such a record shall be made on the custody record when the person occupying or controlling the premises is detained when the record is made. All of which inevitably necessitates you briefing the inspector concerned about the facts underpinning your reasonable suspicion, specifying the evidence you expect to find. In addition the inspector may want to satisfy himself that you have a practical plan of action concerning how, when, and by whom the search is to be carried out, including details of whether or not you intend to take the prisoner with you etc *(see also [D] Conducting a Search of Premises page 114)*.

PACE s10

Note: Items of legal privilege

Items of legal privilege cannot be searched for or seized under this section.

Comment

The key to using these arrest/search powers effectively lies in considering which premises you want to search, and what you intend to search for, then deciding upon what power, if any, you have readily available, or can acquire by means of a warrant *(see table opposite)*.

The following table may assist you by providing a simple overview of the search powers conferred by s18 and 32, of PACE

Enter and Search: s 32	Enter and Search: s 18
Premises on which arrested/ premises visited immediately prior to arrest	Premises occupied by the arrested person/ premises controlled by the arrested person
for evidence of the offence for which arrested	for evidence of that arrestable offence
and seize anything specified in s19 of PACE.	or evidence of some other arrestable offence similar to/or connected to that offence
	and seize the above items.

Remember

Code B specifies 'general considerations', 'seizure and retention of property' and 'action to be taken after searches' which apply to ss 18, and 32 of PACE.

[B] Search under warrant

Though in general, as an officer dealing with drugs offences at street level, you will use the 'ready' powers of entry, search and seizure without warrant contained in ss 17, 18, 19, and 32 of PACE, except in Scotland *(see [A] Searches Without Warrant page 91)*, there may be occasions when you need the more Draconian powers available to you by means of a warrant granted by a Justice of the Peace (or in Scotland, a Justice of the Peace, a Magistrate or a Sheriff).

The key legislation in this area is that of s 23(3) of the Misuse of Drugs Act 1971 and s 15 and s 16 of PACE. [10]

SECTION 23(3) MISUSE OF DRUGS ACT 1971

This section gives officers (working in the police area in which the premises are situated) the power to:

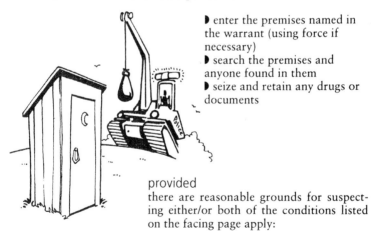

❭ enter the premises named in the warrant (using force if necessary)
❭ search the premises and anyone found in them
❭ seize and retain any drugs or documents

provided
there are reasonable grounds for suspecting either/or both of the conditions listed on the facing page apply:

S

[10] PACE does not apply in Scotland, but s 23 of the Misuse of Drugs Act 1971 does apply and provides the necessary authority for a search under warrant.

❱ an offence has been committed relating to controlled drugs present on the premises or in the possession of anyone in them

❱ any document in possession of a person on the premises is related, or connected, to an actual or intended, unlawful transaction or dealing in drugs (whether in the UK or elsewhere).

Note: Application under oath

Such a warrant may only be granted following an application made under oath, which satisfies the justice of the peace, magistrate, or sheriff that there are reasonable grounds for suspecting that there is a person on the premises who has unlawful possession of a controlled drug.

Note: Accuracy of information and seizure

Be careful when outlining on the warrant what your information says you are likely to recover – be specific. For example. If your information is that you will recover drugs, dealer's records together with money and drug-related paraphernalia, then make sure this is recorded on the warrant.

To simply specify 'controlled drugs together with articles' may cause difficulties later at court when the defence question the issue of articles and what they may or may not be.

When only controlled drugs are mentioned on the warrant and other evidence is also recovered then make sure it is seized under s 19 PACE.

Note: Expiry date

PACE s16 Code B 5.1

The warrant must be executed within one month of the application.

WARRANT

Best Before: 19·6·99

Note: Offences

It is an offence for anyone intentionally to obstruct a person exercising his powers of search (s 23(4) Misuse of Drugs Act 1971). People committing such an offence may of course be arrested, provided that one of the general arrest conditions (s 25 PACE) apply. [11]

S

[11] With regard to the offence of obstruction under s 23(4) of the Misuse of Drugs Act 1971, a Scottish officer derives his power of arrest from s 24 of the same Act which provides:

'A constable may arrest without warrant a person who has committed, or whom the constable, with reasonable cause, suspects to have committed, an offence under the Misuse of Drugs Act 1971 if:

>   (a) he, with reasonable cause, believes that that person will abscond unless arrested; or
>   (b) the name and address of that person are unknown to, and cannot be ascertained by, him, or
>   (c) he is not satisfied that a name and address furnished by that person as his name and address are true.'

S ▶ The power of arrest granted under s 24 of the Act is limited by the conditions laid down in paragraphs (a) to (c) as aforementioned.

However, if the conditions contained in (a) to (c) are not present to justify an arrest under the Act, you may still arrest an accused using your common law powers. (See s 3 of the *Scottish Criminal Law* manual).

Note

In the case of *Carmichael v Brannan* 1985 SCCR 234, it was held that 'obstructs' in s 23(4)(a) of the Act, was not limited to physical obstruction, but covered any act done with intent to hinder officers in the discharge of their duties.

Q. Is it possible to charge a person with obstruction under s 41 of the Police (Scotland) Act 1967 instead of obstruction under s 23(4) of the Misuse of Drugs Act 1971?

A. Yes, provided the provisions contained in s 41 of the Police (Scotland) Act 1967 have been contravened by the accused.

Under Scots law, the question of whether an officer had 'reasonable grounds to suspect' within the context of s 23 of the Misuse of Drugs Act 1971, is a question of law for the judge in any trial involving the use of this power.

Basically this involves the judge considering the fundamental principle of 'fairness to the accused', within the circumstances of the case under review.

SECTIONS 15 AND 16 OF PACE AND CODE B OF THE CODES OF PRACTICE

These impose a series of conditions concerning applying for and executing such warrants which must be complied with. Together they detail the process of:

▶ action to be taken before an application is made
▶ making an application
▶ completing a warrant.

(See also [D] Conducting a Search page 114, and [E] Seizure and Retention of Property page 118.)

[1] ACTION BEFORE AN APPLICATION

Q. What do I need to do before making an application for a search warrant?

| CODE B 2.1 | A. It is vital that you check the information to make sure it is accurate – recent – genuine (ie not made maliciously or irresponsibly). |

Police-Community liason Officer

CODE B 2.4	Remember that an application for a search warrant cannot be made without an inspector's authority – except when no inspector is available and the matter is urgent, in which case the 'senior officer on duty' may authorise an application – so the first thing you must do is convince the inspector, who will expect you to have done your homework and be able to furnish all the necessary information.

CODE B 2.5 and Note 2B	If there is reason to believe that the search could harm community relations, then the police community liaison officer must be consulted – except in cases of urgency where it is possible to take retrospective action by informing both the local police/community liaison officer and any local police/community consultative groups as soon as practicable after the search.

PACE s15 CODE B 2.1-3	The inspector, magistrate or judge will want to know: ▶ what type of drug or drugs are suspected of being on the premises ▶ the location of such evidence (and/or other evidence) ▶ what you know about the likely occupier of the premises ▶ what you know about the premises themselves, and ▶ whether they have been previously searched and, if so, how recently.

Note: Search registers

A check of the relevant premises' search register would indicate whether the premises have recently been searched.

Comment

It is important that we do not discredit ourselves by obtaining warrants on flimsy information and then face further embarrassment by returning unnecessary negative results to the clerk to the justices.

Q. What do I need to do to make an application?

CODE B
2.6

A. The application for a search warrant must be made in writing, specifying:

▶ the legislation relevant to the application (eg s 23(3) Misuse of Drugs Act 1971)
▶ the premises to be searched (ie the full address)
▶ the 'object' of the search (eg to search for a specific drug(s) if known)
▶ the grounds for the application.

Note: Further applications

CODE B
2.8

Once an application has been refused, no further application can be made without 'additional grounds', so it is extremely important to get it right first time.

Note: Informants

CODE B
Note 2A

It is not necessary to name your informant but you may need to discuss previous information from the same source, by way of verification, or indeed answer questions about the accuracy of such previous information *(see also [2] Informants – section H page 132)*.

Comment

When in court, you will be asked questions by the magistrates about your information. It is important not to reveal the contents of your information to anyone other than those required to see it and you should guard against disclosing the address in open court.

Your information is for the magistrate's eyes only. However, be prepared to deal with any questions the court may want to ask about your information. Remember too that colleagues can be careless with information, so share it only with those who need to know about it.

[2] COMPLETING THE WARRANT

Q. What do I do with the warrant after completing the search, or when it has expired?

PACE A s16

A. When a warrant has been executed it must be endorsed to the effect that:

❱ the articles or persons sought were or were not found;
❱ any other articles (other than those sought) were seized.

When a warrant has been executed or not executed (within the time outlined) it must be returned to
either:
the clerk to the justices of the petty sessional area of the issuing justice of the peace;
or
an appropriate officer of the court of the issuing judge.

Note: Retention of warrants
The returned warrants are then retained for 12 months, during which time the occupiers concerned may inspect them.

[C] Search with consent

While considering our different powers of entry to search premises, perhaps we should not overlook the use of consent. Once again an example may help – remember Page?

Example

In interview, Page volunteers the fact that the medical bag itself was concealed under his next-door neighbour's shed.

PACE gives no power to search, but imposes rules as to how the search can be carried out.

| CODE B 4.1 | If practicable a 'notice of powers and rights' must be given to the person (entitled to grant entry to premises) who consents to a search, before the search takes place |

and

| CODE B 4.2 | before asking for consent, the officer in charge must state the purpose and tell the person concerned that they are not obliged to consent; that anything seized may be produced in evidence; and if the person is not suspected of an offence, the officer shall tell them so. |

It is not necessary however to seek consent where this would cause 'disproportionate inconvenience' to the person concerned.

An example of this could be where police have arrested someone in the night after a pursuit and it is necessary to make a brief check of gardens along the route to see whether any drugs have been thrown away

Note: Lodging houses

CODE B
Note 4A

The Codes of Practice advise that when searching lodging houses or similar accommodation, it is necessary to obtain the consent of the landlord, unless the matter is urgent.

Comment

CODE B
4.3

The key point made by the Code of Practice is that when a power of entry exists (either with or without warrant) the co-operation, not the consent, of the appropriate person should be sought; with consent only being sought when no power exists.

Such consent should be both fully informed and freely given and not 'managed' or 'obtained by duress'. What is more, if such consent is refused or withdrawn, the search must not start or continue.

[D] Conducting a search

Q. What are the rules governing the searching of premises?
A. Both PACE and the Codes of Practice lay down rules about the searching of premises. These rules fall into three separate categories:

[1] GENERAL CONSIDERATIONS

PACE s16	CODE B 5.1-2	CODE B note 5A

The search itself must be at a reasonable hour, ideally at a time when the occupier is likely to be there and not asleep (unless this would frustrate the search).

Note: Searches under warrant

CODE B 5.1, 5.3

If the search is made under warrant, it must be conducted within one month of the issue of the warrant and the warrant can only be used once.

[2] COMMUNICATING WITH THE OCCUPIER

PACE
s16
CODE B
5.4-5.5

The officer in charge of the search should explain to the occupier or person in charge of the premises the authority for the search and ask to be allowed into the premises, unless:

❥ the premises are unoccupied
❥ no one is present
❥ communicating with the occupier/person in charge would frustrate the search or endanger the officer, or other people.

[2.i] Notice of powers and rights

Unless not practicable, the officer making the search must give the occupier a copy of the Notice of Powers and Rights before the search begins.

Note: Contents of the Notice of Powers and Rights
The Notice of Powers and Rights must include the following points:

❥ the type of search, ie 'with warrant', 'with consent' or 'following an arrest' and the authority for the search
❥ a summary of the available powers
❥ a summary of the rights of the owner/occupier
❥ an explanation of the means of obtaining compensation for damages
❥ a statement that copies of the Codes of Practice are available at any police station.

[2.ii] Warrants

<table>
<tr><td>PACE
s16
CODE B
5.8</td><td>If practicable, the officer in charge of the search should produce the warrant and give the occupier a copy of it before the search begins. However, if the occupier is not present, a copy – suitably endorsed with the name of the officer in charge, details of the</td></tr>
</table>

officer's police station and the time and date of the search – must be left in a prominent position.

Comment

Copies of the warrant and the Notice of Powers and Rights need not be served on the occupier before the search begins, if the officer believes that doing so would frustrate the search or endanger the officers or other people.

<table>
<tr><td>CODE B
5.9</td><td>The search must only be carried out to the extent necessary to find the object of the search and continue only up to the point when such objects are found, or when the officer in charge is satisfied that they will not be found.</td></tr>
</table>

<table>
<tr><td>CODE B
5.10</td><td>Those undertaking the search must be considerate in respect of property, privacy and the disruption caused by the search. Reasonable force should only be used when the occupier refuses or and is unable to provide sufficient co-operation.</td></tr>
</table>

<table>
<tr><td>CODE B
5.11</td><td>The occupier can ask a friend, neighbour or other person to witness the search and this should only be refused where the officer in charge has reasonable grounds for believing that this would seriously hinder the investigation.</td></tr>
</table>

[3] LEAVING THE PREMISES

CODE B
5.12

Where force has been used to gain entry, the officer in charge is responsible for securing the premises. (Ideally this involves ensuring that the occupier or his agent is present before the police leave.)

Note: The wrong premises

CODE B
and
Note 5C

The Code of Practice even caters for that most embarrassing of situations, searching the wrong premises by mistake. It emphasises that everything possible must be done to make up for the wrong – by apologising and explaining what has happened and by assisting the occupier to obtain compensation.

[E] Seizure/retention of property

Q. What items can I seize in the course of a search of premises?

A. Whether searching premises under a statutory power or with consent, an officer may seize anything:

<table>
<tr><td>CODE B
6.1</td><td>▶ stated in the warrant</td></tr>
</table>

and

<table>
<tr><td>CODE B
6.2</td><td>▶ which there are reasonable grounds for believing to be evidence of an offence or obtained through committing an offence;</td></tr>
</table>

provided

<table>
<tr><td>PACE
s10</td><td>▶ the item is not subject to legal privilege.</td></tr>
</table>

Note: Property not seized

<table>
<tr><td>CODE B
6.3</td><td>Although there are reasonable grounds for believing that an item has been obtained in consequence of committing an offence, the officer may decide it is not necessary to seize it because, for example, it was stolen property, bought for 'value in and good faith'. However the officer must inform the 'holder' of this and warn him that he must return the property, or face possible civil or criminal proceedings. Such an instance, however, is hardly likely in relation to drugs searches.</td></tr>
</table>

Note: Copying information and computer records

<table>
<tr><td>CODE B
6.5</td><td>When making such a search an officer can photograph or copy anything which could be seized and require computer disks or print-out, etc as evidence.</td></tr>
</table>

Q. How long can the police retain the property seized in a search?

CODE B
6.6

A. The simple answer is 'as long is necessary', given that it may be retained:

❱ for use as evidence at a trial
❱ for forensic examination or other investigation
❱ to establish the lawful owner.

(Note that property cannot be retained, if a photograph or copy would serve the same purpose.)

Q. What right do the owners of property 'seized' have in relation to it?

CODE B
6.8-6.9
and
Note 6A

A. The rights of the person who had custody-control prior to seizure are twofold:

❱ the right to have a list or description of the property (within a reasonable time)
❱ the right for themselves or their representative to have supervised access, to examine the property, or have it copied or photographed (within a reasonable time and at their own expense), unless the officer in charge of the investigation has reasonable grounds for believing that this would prejudice the investigation or criminal proceedings, in which case the grounds for refusal must be recorded.

Note: Provision of the Police (Property) Act 1897

Persons claiming property seized by the police should be advised of their right to apply to a magistrates' court for possession.

Comment

Remember that drugs dealers sometimes accept goods in lieu of money for drugs and may actually live in somewhere akin to the fabled 'Aladdin's cave'.

[F] Action after searches

Q. What records do I have to make after completing a search?
    A. There are three records which may require completion, these being:

[1.i] The search record

CODE B
7.1

The search record will include –the address of the premises, the time/date/duration of the search – the authority and power (where applicable) – a copy of the warrant or written consent (where applicable) – the names of those involved – the names of the people on the premises (where known) – a list of the items seized (or place where it can be found) – the reason for the seizure (where applicable) the fact and reason for the seizure – details of any damage and the circumstances of how it was caused.

[1.ii] The warrant (where applicable)

CODE B
7.2

This will be endorsed with – whether the articles specified were found – any other articles seized – the date/time it was executed – the names of the officers involved – information concerning the method of supplying with the copy warrant and Notice of Powers and Rights.

Note: Returning warrant

CODE B
7.3

(See [B] Searches Under Warrant page 104, regarding the procedure for retaining used or time expired warrants.)

[1.iii] The premises searched register

CODE B 8.1

This must be maintained at all divisional/sub-divisional stations as – a central reference point in which all the records required under this Code must be: made – copied – referred to.

Note: Section 18 searches

Remember also the need to record the authority for a s 18 search of premises following an arrest for an arrestable offence, (which may be entered on the custody record where the arrested person is in custody).

[G] Practical tips

We have looked at the many and varied powers available to you, the police officer, when searching premises and seizing evidence. Now it is time to mention some practical issues which, if considered properly from the outset, may prove as important as having knowledge of your powers.

The following practical tips may be of use to those involved in, or supervising the investigation process.

[1] SEARCHING

Many factors will dictate the manner of search and these will include:

- ❱ location of premises
- ❱ type and size of premises
- ❱ numbers of person present at the premises
- ❱ resources available
- ❱ previous history of premises
- ❱ knowledge of occupants.

[2] GATHERING INFORMATION

It is essential that you gather as much information as possible about the premises, its lay-out and the location of outer doors. All possibilities must be planned for, with windows and doors being observed while the warrant is being executed in case evidence is thrown from them. It is not uncommon for drugs to be flushed down toilets when entry is made and it may even be worth considering 'bagging' the drains which service them (ie putting a large polythene bag over the outlet pipe to catch anything flushed away). A plan of the premises may be available and can be used to direct officers to specific points and tasks.

Consider this checklist when preparing to search premises:

▶ What are the premise like?
▶ What do I know about the occupants?
▶ How am I going to get inside?
▶ How many people are likely to be there?
▶ Will there be a dog on the premises?

(A large net is often useful in ensuring that dogs do not present a risk to officers.)

▶ Will there be children present?
▶ How many officers will be needed?
▶ How should they be deployed?
▶ When is the best time to enter the premises?
▶ What drug or drugs are suspected?
▶ Should I use a drugs dog?
▶ Who will look after the exhibits?
▶ To which police station or stations will any prisoners be taken? (Remember to let them know of the likelihood of extra prisoners before the operation).
▶ Who will interview the prisoners?

The method of entry will also need to be carefully considered as the use of force is not always the best option. Sometimes subterfuge is the most successful method of gaining entry into a premise, or at least getting the occupant to open the door. This means of entry is particularly useful if children live there and is an added safeguard to prevent people being injured unnecessarily. A decided case may help to reassure you concerning the desirability of using subterfuge.

Note: *R v Longman* (1988) 1 WLR 619

Drugs officers having previously experienced difficulty in gaining entry to premises, executed a warrant by having an officer pose as an Interflora delivery agent. It was held that under the circumstances it was permissible to gain entry and then identify oneself and produce the warrant once entry was gained (*See Code B, 5.4 and 5.5*).

[3] BRIEFING FOR A SEARCH

It is also extremely important to hold a thorough briefing for all concerned to make sure all those involved are aware of their role and responsibilities no matter how big or small the operation is.

The following points may assist you to carry out a professional and informative briefing:

Search briefing checklist

▶ Prepare adequately for the briefing.
▶ Make sure everyone is present.
▶ Use aids to assist in your explanation of what is required, such as
- maps
- plans
- video footage
- photographs.

▶ Get people to make notes.
▶ Cover all the angles.
▶ Assign clear roles and responsibilities to each individual (remember to appoint an exhibits officer).
▶ Ensure that everyone is clear on the specific legal and practical points associated with a drugs search, ie obstruction (s 23 of the Misuse of Drugs Act); unsolicited comments; questioning which could amount to an interview (Code C, Codes of Practice).
▶ Review the briefing to make sure the information has been fully understood.
▶ Remember to do a 'hot wash-up' after the operation, de-briefing carefully and constructively what went right, wrong and what you would change with hindsight.

This is extremely important for the success of future operations.

During the briefing, the rules of searching should be explained as follows:

Rules of search checklist

▶ Once entered, the premises should be controlled.
▶ All rooms thoroughly checked for occupants.
▶ Maintain order, ensuring any distractions such as television sets etc are turned off.

▶ Identify the occupants and give them a copy of the search warrant (if applicable) together with the Notice of Powers and Rights.
▶ People should be searched first – with females being searched by females, and males by males.
▶ Once searched they should be watched carefully and not allowed to wander around.

[4] CONDUCTING THE SEARCH

A systematic search should be made of the premises

Conducting the search checklist

▶ If a drugs dog is available and is required to search, it should be allowed to do so before the rooms are disturbed.

▶ Ideally two officers should search a room in the presence of the occupiers, who should be accompanied by a third officer. The search should be carried out in tidy fashion with items removed from drawers and cupboards and replaced after examination. A system of searching is the best way of operating, with each officer having half the room to search. When they have searched their half of the room they then cross over and check the half searched by their colleague. That way the room is effectively searched twice.

▶ Any suspect substances should be shown to the occupier and any comment recorded contemporaneously and the record offered for reading and signing, but this must not develop into an impromptu interview without the benefit of legal advice. Substances and other exhibits should be handed to the exhibits officer who should label them and note where and by whom they were recovered.

Remember

It is good to make recoveries of drugs, but seemingly innocent articles may be of great evidential value. Consider seizing:

> ▶ scraps of paper containing names, telephone numbers and lists of transactions which may show evidence of dealing – these may prove valuable in interview

> ▶ address books – entries in relation to known drug abusers may reveal interesting links or indicate a source of supply

> ▶ correspondence – drug users tend to reveal habits in letters to each other

> ▶ photographs – these may show an association with other drug users and suppliers.

❱ money (large amounts which cannot legitimately be accounted for may be the proceeds of drug dealing).

❱look for items which indicate drug abuse or drug dealing and seize them, they may be the evidence you require.

[4.i] Signs of Drug Abuse

Signs of drug abuse checklist

Item	Drug
❱ Paper folds/wraps	Amphetamine, Cocaine, Heroin
❱ Syringes/tourniquets spoons with charring under the bowl	Amphetamine, Heroin, etc, (injection)
❱ Citric acid or lemon juice	Heroin (injection)
❱ Drinking straw or rolled bank notes	Cocaine (snorting)
❱ Bicarbonate of soda, home made pipes or perforated drinks cans	Crack cocaine (smoking)
❱ Stained and charred cooking foil, cardboard or cooking foil tubes	Heroin (smoking)
❱ Hand rolled cigarettes or cigarette ends with rolled cardboard filters. Large home made pipes, ornamental hookah pipes (smelling of 'smoking'), torn Rizla packets	Cannabis resin (or Cannabis)
❱ Mirrors, razor blades	Any powdered drugs

[4.ii] Signs of Possible Drug Dealing

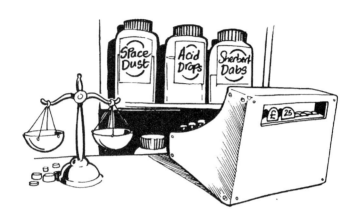

Signs of drug dealing checklist

Item	Drug
▶ Boxed brass scales usually with purple or red velvet covering, or electric scales	Any drug – most commonly Amphetamine, Cannabis Resin or both
▶ Brass letter scales on a wooden base	Any drug
▶ 'Finger scales' (D-shaped hung from a finger and having a clip for substance being weighed)	Cannabis Resin
▶ Glossy magazines, cooking foil, cling film, bank coin bags and small polythene bags	Any drug

[5] SEARCH OF LICENSED PREMISES

Because of the type of premises involved, it is rare that good results follow searches of licensed premises. Drugs are often disposed of as officers enter the premises and, while drugs are quite often recovered, it is difficult to establish who is responsible. Operations can be mounted and evidence gathered which may be used to prove offences by managers of those premises *(see Chapter 7)*.

[6] ILLICIT LABORATORIES

You will be aware that cannabis is often grown in the UK, sometimes on quite a large scale. There have been instances of laboratories synthesising LSD and other substances although heroin,
cocaine and cannabis are usually produced abroad.

It is not everyday that you will stumble upon an illicit laboratory but they are likely to be situated in a house, or can be set up
in out-houses or industrial premises, with some sophisticated
equipment being used. Depending on how the laboratory has
been revealed will dictate how you may react. If the laboratory is
identified from information received there will be an opportunity
to prepare a plan of action. This will usually involve several
stages and will necessitate forensic scientists being used to provide advice and valuable evidence.

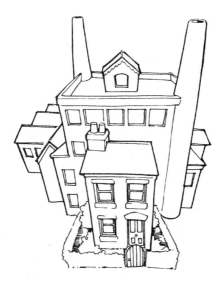

Note:
A useful guide to the assistance provided by the Forensic Science
Service is contained in the Appendices to the *Drugs Workshop
Manual* published by the ACPO Drugs Sub Committee.

Q. What are these stages likely to be?

A. ▶ Preliminary intelligence – no matter how the information has been obtained, or from whom, scientific advice will be required.

▶ Planning the raid – timing is all important but may be difficult to determine. Scientists will continue to work with officers to assess and advise.

▶ Proper action at scene – investigating officers must enter premises swiftly to detain persons present while forensic scientists ensure the safety of the scene.

▶ Product and equipment analysis – the examination and analysis of items recovered will be carried out by forensic scientists.

▶ Preparing the statements – well recorded statements will be required from all officers in attendance. The statements from the forensic scientists will provide the important information which will tend to confirm or otherwise your initial information.

Q. What if I stumble across an illicit laboratory?

A. Well, clearly the circumstances of you finding the laboratory may force your hand. But remember, whatever is decided you must involve the forensic science service as soon as possible.

If you find such a laboratory remember:

▶ don't smoke – many chemicals used are highly flammable

▶ don't touch things – they may be contaminated with acids or harmful substances

▶ don't turn off water supplies – this may be used to cool a chemical reaction and turning them off may have an adverse effect.

Remember
Dealing with illicit laboratories is a highly specialised matter and requires specialist knowledge which should be arranged through a senior officer.

[H] Other search considerations

In this final section we shall cover the issue of two classes of person who need special protection and whom we sometimes overlook when searching premises. They are children and informants.

[1] PROTECTING CHILDREN

The risks to children who live with drug abusers are not always recognised, but where recoveries of drugs or drug-related items such as needles and syringes are made in premises where children live, this information must be brought to the attention of the Social Services Department.

One way of doing this is by completing a form, that may be in place in your force, which suggests that a child is, or may be in trouble or at risk. The form is often routed through a Juvenile Liaison Officer, or equivalent, to the Social Services Department who can use this information either as a preventive measure or to build up a picture of the child and family. Your information could help to save a child's life.

[2] INFORMANTS

When properly used, informants are an essential aid to criminal investigation and this is particularly true in respect of drugs. Strict guidelines exist in relation to the registration and subsequent contact with informants, calling for sound ethical and professional judgment. It is important that police officers observe the policies and rules associated with informants and ensure they are strictly complied with. To do otherwise could place both the informant and you in jeopardy.

(See Home Office Circular 97/1969, the Drug Workshop Manual *produced by the ACPO Drugs Sub-Committee and your own Force Policy on this issue.)*

Chapter 6

GATHERING & SAFEGUARDING EVIDENCE

INTRODUCTION

The investigation of drug-related offences is no different to the investigation of other crime. The rules are the same in that any evidence must be properly and fairly obtained, correctly documented and safeguarded to prevent allegations that the police have acted improperly. Such allegations could have serious implications for those involved in the investigative process, as well as losing the job at court. In the simplest of drugs investigations there may be numerous exhibits which collectively complete a jigsaw. If part of the jigsaw is lost then the picture is incomplete. This is how a court will see a case with part of the evidence missing.

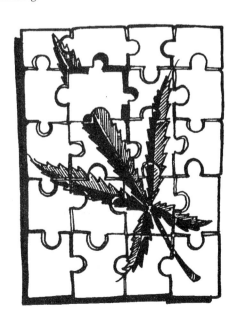

In this chapter we will look at the procedures which follow a successful job and require careful attention to safeguard the evidence. We will concentrate on:

S Officers serving in the Scottish Police Forces should refer to their own force's *Standing Orders* or *Procedures Manual* for guidance on the matters raised by this chapter, because there may be minor differences in procedures between the eight Scottish Police Forces. However, you are likely to find the contents of this chapter both interesting and useful from a practical point of view.

[A] Safeguarding initial recoveries

In all investigations it feels good to get a result and it is satisfying to recover drugs and evidence after a lengthy operation involving careful planning, numerous briefings, (just as many de-briefings), the staffing of observation points and the occasional unexpected hitch. However, many outstanding seizures result from officers carrying out their routine day-to-day duties. The circumstances and nature of the job will largely dictate whether you will deal with the job from start to finish, or whether it will be passed to a specialist unit. Quite often Force Drugs Squads through necessity, are fully committed to large scale investigations, which take them away from local work. In these instances the officer making the initial recovery may have to take the case through to its conclusion. Whoever deals with the job the initial recovery is vitally important.

Q. How can I safeguard my initial recovery?

A. By sealing it in a tamper evident bag, in the presence of the suspect, so that allegations of mishandling cannot be made. An example may help, so lets look again at Page:

Example

You are on patrol and have reliable information from a tried and tested source that Page is in possession of some cannabis resin. Seeing Page in the street you exercise your search powers under s 23(2) Misuse of Drugs Act, 1971 (*see Chapter 4*) and recover an 'eighth' from his jacket pocket. If you are in possession of a polythene tamper evident bag, with a self sealing device, incorporating an exhibit label and a unique serial number, you will be able to seal the drug at the time of seizure and have Page sign the seal. If he refused to sign you can endorse the seal accordingly.

Q. When I recover substances I usually keep them in my pocket until I get to the Police Station. Then I seal them properly in the interview. What is wrong with doing that?

A. Your Force may have a policy on the way drugs are recovered and you must be guided by that, but in addition we suggest the following 'good practice'. Let's return to 'Page'.

Example

Imagine the cannabis taken from Page was put into your pocket to be sealed later but, while showing it to the custody officer, Page either grabs and swallows it, or suggests that the piece of cannabis taken from him was bigger than the piece you have produced. He says you must have taken some of the cannabis before it was produced to the custody officer. These problems could also occur during the interview, so avoid unnecessary complaints and safeguard your evidence by placing it in the tamper evident bag at the time of seizure.

Q. The tamper evident bags you describe sounds excellent, but try finding one when you need one! What do you do then?

A. The answer is to get one before you need it and carry it with you. There are at least two sizes of tamper evident bags and the smaller one is particularly useful for street recoveries. Have one handy in your pocket or brief case, but if this proves difficult all is not lost. Simply carry a manilla envelope (preferably with a 'window') and use this to make your initial recovery safe. This is how it works:

Example

When you recover the cannabis from Page, you can place it in the manilla envelope, seal it and have him sign across the seal. At the police station the custody officer will be able to see the evidence through the window of the envelope and the opportunity for Page to swallow the drug, or make allegations is dramatically reduced. The envelope can then be placed unopened straight into a tamper evident bag to safeguard continuity.

Q. What if Page was obstructive or violent and I was unable to seal the drug at the time of initial recovery?

A. Well clearly you are going to prioritise and safeguard the evidence as best you can. The fact that Page was difficult can be brought out in interview and may even go some way to providing evidence of obstruction (s 23(4) Misuse of Drugs Act, 1971) if that was the case.

Note: Safeguarding your recovery

Whenever possible substances suspected of being controlled drugs should be recovered in the presence of the suspect or, in the absence of the suspect, an independent person. Where either course is impractical, more than one police officer should ideally be present.

[B] Protecting your evidence

Having dealt correctly with the initial seizure, it is important to safeguard the drugs and any other evidence you have found.

Q. How can I protect my seizure?
A. Look at the recovery of cannabis from Page and all the things that could go wrong between seizing it and the case appearing at court. The danger of mishandling drugs and not being able to account for their movement is very real.

Remember danger signs:

- don't leave drugs unattended
- don't put drugs in your pockets, locker or drawers
- document the recovery as soon as possible

Let's look at Page again to highlight the point.

Example

Upon arrest you find that Page is drunk and the custody officer considers him unfit for interview. Knowing you are off duty shortly your supervisor tells you to prepare a statement of recovery and leave the job for the early turn shift. You prepare your written statement and because you feel that the interviewing officer will need to show the cannabis to Page, you do not seal it before putting it in the safe. This is bad practice. Not only is it easy to make allegations of a serious nature it is bad for continuity and the defence could quite easily allege that the substance recovered from Page was not that produced in interview. Always deal with drugs correctly.

Remember

> **S**earch **S**eize **S**eal **S**ecure **S**afely

Q. What 'other' evidence could there be in the example of Page?
A. It is essential to take possession of other things which appear to be evidence of an offence and deal with them properly. These may include:

- drugs paraphernalia
- lists of names
- telephone numbers
- money (including bank/building society books, etc)
- details of transactions
- unsolicited comments.

| CODE |
| C |

Comment

The rules for dealing with any unsolicited comments are contained in the Codes of Practice.

Example

> At the time of recovering the cannabis from Page's jacket pocket he says to you: 'It's just a bit of dope for my own use. I bought it from a man in a pub.' Provided no questions, *which could amount to an interview*, have been asked, this would be an important unsolicited comment.

Q. How and when will this unsolicited comment be introduced in evidence?

| CODE |
| C |
| 11.2A |

A. The comment amounts to a significant statement which occurred before Page arrived at the police station and would need to be put to him at the beginning of the interview after caution. Make sure you comply with the Codes of Practice and protect your evidence *(see Chapter 7)*.

[C] Packaging, exhibiting recoveries and documentation; plus dealing with cannabis plants

[1] PACKAGING DRUGS

Later in this chapter we will cover drugs identification, or examination for evidential purposes, but it will save time if the drugs are correctly packaged from the outset. Where there is only one substance involved, as in the example of Page, there is no real problem as long as it is packaged correctly. However, there are additional considerations when more than one type of drug is recovered and it makes sense to package them separately. Remember too, that in Scotland, Forces may have dedicated or shared laboratories, so it is vitally important for officers in Scotland to read this section in conjunction with their own Force procedures.

Example

> If Page had been in possession of a bag of heroin and some loose tablets in addition to the cannabis mentioned earlier, think ahead about the problems of subsequent identification *(see [F] Identification of Cannabis)*. The bag of heroin and the tablets are more likely to be sent to the Forensic Science Laboratory for analysis then the cannabis. Each type of drug would in fact have a separate police item number *(see [2] Exhibiting Recoveries)* and should be packaged separately.

[2] EXHIBITING RECOVERIES

The officer who recovers the substance must make sure that the item is correctly identified and be specific about both the contents of seizure and items forwarded for examination.

Example

> If PC Cross had been the officer recovering these drugs from Page then the drugs would assume the police item number RC1, RC2 and RC3. However, when PC Cross recovers the bank bag, containing the heroin from Page and documents it as police item RC1, imagine the concern when the bag is examined at the Forensic Science Laboratory and, in addition to the heroin, is found to contain a wrap of amphetamine and another smaller piece of cannabis resin. If checked properly this recovery would have amounted to three exhibits instead of one.

Note

People acting as exhibit officers may have different views on multiple recoveries and anomalies for sequencing exist. In difficult situations it is wise to consult with the CPS.

Q. What about the other evidence recovered from Page?

A. The list of names, telephone numbers, details of transactions and the money would also assume consecutive police item numbers using the initials of the officer recovering, and introducing them into evidence.

Comment

Some of the items recovered may not be relevant to the final charges and while it is important that they are all given police item numbers it can be difficult for the Crown Prosecution Service to decide whether or not they are relevant when they have not been properly described on exhibit labels. It is also important to describe them fully in your statement.

[3] DOCUMENTATION

Force guidelines concerning the proper documentation of drugs recoveries vary considerably. Some forces maintain Divisional, Sub-Divisional or Sector registers (which are used solely for drug recoveries ie, drug registers), while others may simply use property registers

Whatever system is used the important thing is to enter them carefully, recording the weights and quantities, together with details of the recovery, ie where from, who from, by whom etc.

Comment
Some people will enter all the drugs recovered on one property entry. However this can cause problems.

Example

The heroin seized from Page will have to be shown in interview, identified by presumptive testing, perhaps sent to the Laboratory, exhibited at court, plus any re-packaging or weighing. All of which activities would require separate entries on the property record to account for its movement. Multiply this by the number of drugs seized from Page and you can begin to imagine how complicated that record is, raising the possibility of error.

We suggest that you record each drug on a separate record to keep things simple.

Q. What about other seized items which will not be required for analysis?

A. It makes sense to enter things, like the list of names, telephone numbers, transactions and money together in a completely separate entry to keep things straightforward. This advice may prove useful when later, innocent articles have to be returned to suspects, or we are seeking to secure the forfeiture of money or property *(see Chapter 7)*, or when asking the court to make destruction orders in respect of associated items such as scales and pipes etc.

[4] DEALING WITH CANNABIS PLANTS

Care has to be taken when cannabis plants are recovered as they should not be sealed into polythene bags. If plants are packaged this way they will sweat, rot and quickly turn to a nasty smelling liquid mush.

Q. How should I deal with 'jobs' involving cannabis plants?
A. Perhaps an example, using Page again, may help:

Example

Imagine, during the search of Page's house, you find four healthy mature cannabis plants growing in pots on the sideboard and a further six smaller cannabis plants (seedlings) growing in pots in the airing cupboard. You see that the airing cupboard, which has been whitewashed, is equipped with make-shift electrical lighting strips hanging from the ceiling. Near to the plants there is a small watering can and a bottle of plant food.

In this example there is an abundance of evidence which if used properly will go a long way towards proving offences. Ideally you should:

> ▶ Get a Scenes of Crime officer to the premises to photograph all of the plants and the arrangements inside the airing cupboard.

❱ Seize the lighting strips, watering can, plant food and any other items associated with the offence. (TAKE CARE WITH MAKESHIFT ELECTRIC EQUIPMENT AND SEEK ASSISTANCE WHERE NECESSARY.)

❱ Remove all the plants from the pots and get rid of the soil from the roots.

❱ Keep the most mature plant from your recovery separate from the others and place it in a manilla envelope, bag or sack (not polythene) depending on its size. Attach an exhibit label to the sealed bag and enter it in the property register. This will be your exhibit for the forensic science Laboratory if required.

❱ Place the remaining nine plants into another manilla bag and enter them into the property register as a second separate item, giving them a consecutive number.

Note

Always check your own force policy, regarding the recovery of evidence connected with drugs related offences. This is particularly necessary for officers serving in Scotland. *(See [F] page 150 regarding the identification of cannabis plants.)*

[D] Continuity of evidence

The 'chain of recovery' is one of the most important pieces of evidence and is often overlooked. You may not fully appreciate the consequences of the defence being able to show that the chain of recovery was broken. How would you feel if a case was lost due to a break in continuity, with the defence able to suggest that the substance recovered from the suspect was not that actually analysed at the laboratory.

It is vital that everyone who 'handles' the substance makes a statement outlining the purpose of their possession of it. Let's consider what the continuity chain could include:

> ❱ A statement from the officer who recovers the drug at the scene and hands it to the exhibits officer. (State identification number.)

> ❱ A statement from the exhibits officer receiving the drug from the recovering officer and then handing it over to the interviewing officer to use in the interview. (State identification number.)

> ❱ A statement from the interviewing officer receiving the drug and sealing it during interview and, after interview, placing the bag containing the drug in the 'property' store. (State identification number.)

> ❱ A statement from the person who removes the bag from the property store and hands it to the person who then transports it to the Forensic Science Laboratory. (State identification number.)

> ❱ A statement from the person who transports the substance to the Forensic Science Laboratory or Scottish equivalent. (State identification number.)

> ❱ A statement from the person who brings the substance from the Laboratory and returns it to the property officer. (State identification number.)

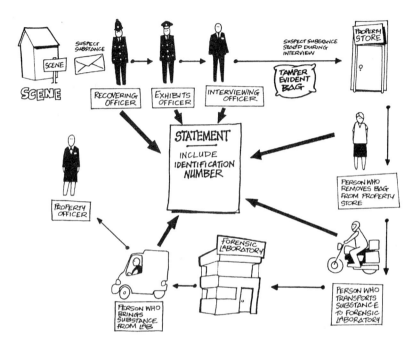

Comment

Of course you would also receive a statement of evidence in due course from the Forensic Scientist Laboratory analysing the substance who would also make reference to the relevant identification number. On many occasions drugs are removed from the property store for the purpose of presumptive testing. This should also be covered in statements.

You can see how easy it is to miss out a statement and break the chain of continuity. As the officer in the case it is your responsibility to make sure the chain is strong and unbroken and one way of doing this is to limit the number of people involved in handling the substance. Another thing to do is to reconstruct the chain yourself to ensure that there are no missing links. You may even feel it appropriate to prepare a schedule outlining all the links in the chain.

[E] Presumptive testing and the use of results in proceedings

Presumptive testing is a means of obtaining a speedy identification of a drug. Let's look at the process:

Q. I thought all suspected drugs had to be sent to the Forensic Science Laboratory for analysis?

A. No, some drugs can be 'presumptive tested'. Providing the seizure is either amphetamine, heroin or morphine, it can be tested locally by the police using a Home Office approved drug testing kit operated by a suitably qualified person.

Q. When can a presumptive test be used?

A. The testing kit can be used in the following circumstances:

> ▶ In guilty pleas at Magistrates' Court where the defendant admits the possession
>
> and
>
> confirms the type of drug, before being told the result of the test
>
> and
>
> states it is for personal use
>
> and
>
> the quantity of the drug is small (ie for personal use).

> ▶ (Where the above criteria apply) but the defendant is then committed to a Crown Court for sentence.

> ▶ For remand in custody or conditional bail. (In which case it is not necessary to meet the criteria set out above. However analysis at the Forensic Science Laboratory will still be required for court purposes.)

Let's re-visit Page again to make this clear:

S

> In Scotland, in respect of Presumptive Testing, Forensic examination and packaging of drugs, it is imperative that you check your own force procedures. This is important because some forces have their own laboratories while others share their facilities with other forces.

Example

When interviewed, Page admits that he is in possession of a small amount of amphetamine which is for his own use. If the recovery is such that this is a reasonable account, and provided that its possession and identity was admitted by Page before he was given the result, a presumptive test could be carried out. On the other hand, had Page been found in possession of a large amount of the drug; admitted supplying the drug; or denied identity or possession of it, then presumptive testing can only be carried out for a remand in custody, or for conditional bail. The substance must then be sent to the Forensic Science Laboratory (except Scotland) for analysis before trial.

Q. Which samples must be sent to the Lab for forensic examination?
A. Samples must always be sent to the Forensic Science Laboratory if any of the following circumstances apply:

> ❱ the result of a test does not support the admissions
> ❱ the admission of possession or identity is withdrawn
> ❱ the case is to be dealt with at the Crown Court (for other than sentencing).

Examples

If Page admits possession of a substance which he states categorically is heroin (emphasising that the small amount was for his personal use) but, when tested, it appears that the substance may be something other than heroin;

or

if, after admitting possession of amphetamine, Page changes his mind and either retracts his initial admission that the substance was amphetamine or denies possession of it then the substance must go to the Laboratory;

or

if Page was already appearing at the Crown Court for a number of serious offences and the case involving the amphetamine was transferred to that venue, being subsidiary to these other offences,   then

the substance would need to be analysed at the Laboratory.

[F] Identification of cannabis

Q. When can cannabis be identified without being sent for analysis to the Laboratory?
A. Forensic analysis of cannabis – including cannabis resin but not hash oil *(see facing page)* – is not required in cases dealt with at a Magistrates Court where an officer trained to identify it (by its appearance, texture and odour) states that the drug is cannabis provided:

> ❱ the person pleads guilty
>> and
> ❱ the person admits possession and that it is cannabis
>> and
> ❱ it is for personal use
>> and
> ❱ it is a small amount consistent with personal use.

Note: Crown Prosecution Service

This means of identification may also be accepted by the Crown Prosecution Service where:

> ❱ the criteria outlined above apply but the defendant is committed for sentence to the Crown Court
>> or
> ❱ a remand in custody is sought or conditional bail is granted.

However, forensic analysis will be necessary if the case is to be tried at the Crown Court.

Q. Who can identify cannabis under these circumstances?

A. This is very much down to individual Force policy and the criteria that Chief Officers set. Police officers with at least 12 months' drug squad experience are often regarded as being capable of identifying cannabis because of the regularity they come into contact with it and the knowledge they possess. Remember you must follow your force policy.

Q. Can hash oil be identified by such officers?

A. No, because its not easily identified and recoveries should be sent to the Forensic Science Laboratory for analysis *(see Chapter 2 – Class B Note: Cannabis oil).*

Q. What about Cannabis plants? How can they de identified?

A. Cannabis plants appear to be outside the terms of the 'Guilty Plea' policy and should generally be sent to the Forensic Laboratory for analysis. However, examination of the plants by an experienced drugs squad officer in the first instance may indicate the likely result.

Q. What is meant by the terms 'small quantity' and 'consistent with' personal use?

A. These expressions are important when considering the criteria for identification and for presumptive testing. Each case should be looked at on its merits. Let's return to Page:

S

Once again the position in Scotland appears varied and it will be necessary for officers serving in Scotland to check their own Force procedures.

Example

> The cannabis found in Page's possession is a very 'small amount' and would be 'consistent with personal use'. If he indicated he was going to smoke it himself, this account could be easily accepted when considering the guilty plea policy. However, a heavy smoker of cannabis could possess substantially more of the drug which may still be for 'personal use' and not intended for supply. Quite often the circumstances of the seizure will provide evidence to either support or contradict those terms.

For further information on drug identification, see Home Office Circular 63/1995 which provides advice on the need for forensic analysis of substances suspected to be controlled drugs, the circumstances in which drug testing may be undertaken by police officers, the use of drug testing kits and their results in prosecution.

Note: Monitoring Crack

It is important to be aware that all potential cocaine seizures are to be submitted to your Home Office Forensic Science Laboratory. Such seizures should be clearly documented as 'Potential Crack'. For further information on the monitoring of crack please see Home Office Circular 9/1990. Remember that procedures differ in Scotland and officers should take account of this.

Comment

The forensic scientists are also able to support evidence through the use of 'comparison techniques' – ie linking items and thus individuals and locations together – and 'chemical profiling' – ie comparing samples of drugs objectively.

Advice on both 'comparison techniques' and 'chemical profiling' is contained in the Appendices of the *Drugs Workshop Manual*, produced by the ACPO Drugs Sub Committee.

[G] Test purchases

Another means of gaining evidence is by way of 'test purchases' carried out by plain clothed police officers, and often filmed on video, not as an end in themselves but by way of supporting evidence. The officers operate within a close but covert cover umbrella, to minimise risk and reduce stress.

▶ Such purchases are fraught with possible danger and **must** follow national guidelines and force procedures absolutely.

▶ Both the process and the offences concerned should be closely monitored and supervised to ensure nothing goes wrong.

▶ A full record must be kept of all aspects of the test purchase.

▶ Welfare is also an issue, and officers need to be monitored and supported both during and after such operations.

▶ Before embarking on such a scheme, officers must be trained and must obtain the necessary permission from an officer of at least the rank of Superintendent.

▶ The operation must be supervised directly by an officer not below Detective Inspector rank.

Comment
Officers should also familiarise themselves with the following documents for guidance:

▶ *The Drugs Workshop Manual* – ACPO Drugs Sub Committee

▶ *HO Circular 97/1969* – *Participating Informants*

▶ *HO Circular 97/1969* – *Participation Guidelines*

▶ ACPO (Crime) Letter – *Managing Test Purchases*

▶ *R v Bryce, 1992* – decided case.

Conclusion
The advice contained in this chapter represents the best practice revealed by our researches using a variety of sources, both legal and practical and should be considered alongside your own Force policies. Hopefully our advice and examples will form a basis for your own best practice and give you 'instant experience'.

Chapter 7

PLANNING AND PREPARING FOR THE INTERVIEW

INTRODUCTION

Remember the old adage 'failing to plan is planning to fail'? This is never more true than in a drug interview. If you don't do your homework you are likely to be trounced in interview – or worse find out in court that you missed a vital question when the accused produces his defence like a rabbit out of a hat. This chapter is intended to provide information, advice and ideas about how to plan and prepare for a drugs interview.

S With regard to this chapter, officers serving in a Scottish police force are reminded that their actions, with regard to the interviewing of suspects and/or accused persons, are not governed by the provisions of PACE and the Codes of Practice. Instead they should consult s6 of the *Scottish Criminal Law* manual and their own force's *Standing Orders* or *Procedures Manual* with regard to the questioning of suspects, etc.

The parts of the chapter dealing with 'points to prove' in connection with the Misuse of Drugs Act 1971 and related legislation apply to Scotland and you should find the contents very informative. However, you are reminded that the English 'case decisions' mentioned in the text, may not have been adopted into Scots Law.

In this chapter we will describe the 'best practice' in planning, preparing and conducting a drugs interview, as well as listing the 'points to prove' in relation to all the main drugs offences, and defining drug trafficking. We have also included practical tips in relation to what to do about drugs trafficking and 'exhibiting' in interview. The chapter is formatted as follows:

[A] Planning

Q. What is the aim of the drugs interview?
A. Obviously this will largely depend upon the offences concerned and the evidence available. The first thing to do is review the case and decide what you want to achieve in interview. It may be that, for example in a case of simple possession, you think you have all the evidence and your objective is to introduce it *(see [C] Exhibits page 178)* and give the suspect the opportunity to comment. Or it may be that, in an offence of possession with intent to supply, your purpose is to prove or disprove that suspect's involvement by finding out about their intent, given what you already know.

Q. What are the objectives of the interview?
A. Having decided your overall aim and the probable offence involved, you must decide upon a clear set of objectives which will form the basis of your interview agenda. This will involve three stages:

> ▶ Reviewing all the possible offences, researching their individual points to prove and considering all the defences open to the suspect. (In this case all you have to do is read off the relevant 'points to prove' and 'defences' *(see [B] Points to Prove and [7] Statutory Defences).*
> ▶ Reviewing the existing evidence and deciding how you are going to use it *(see [C] Exhibits).* Then determine what gaps, inconsistencies or weaknesses there are in the evidence, and decide what evidence, explanation or clarification you want from the suspect.
> ▶ Obtaining all the additional background information you can concerning:
>> – the evidence – in reports, statements, photographs, exhibits, expert advice, presumptive testing *(see Chapter 6)* etc
>> – the scene – visit the scene, find out who owns it, what is the suspect's connection with the premises, who else was present, etc
>> – the suspect – previous offending history, involvement in the drugs scene, associates, economic circumstances, etc.

Q. What aspects of PACE should I consider before going into interview?
A. There are number of specific sections of PACE and the Codes of Practice which are relevant to your forthcoming interviews. Here are a few suggested areas of concern:

CODE C 12.3 Note 12B

▶ **Fitness for interview** – Is the person fit for interview? Remember that the custody officer may not be fully aware of the circumstances concerning your prisoner, particularly if the suspect has taken drugs immediately before, or some time prior to, arrest.

CODE C 12.2, 12.7 Note 12C

▶ **The need for rest** – Has the person had sufficient rest, had a meal, or had a break prior to the interview? Once again it is worth checking with custody staff what sleep/meals the prisoner has been given, bearing in mind that the suspect's lifestyle might differ considerably from that of the average person.

CODE C 15

▶ **Reviews?** – Is a review due? If so it would be advisable to have their review take place before going into the interview.

PACE s31

▶ **Notional arrest?** – Has the person been notionally arrested for any further offences since their original arrest? Perhaps having reviewed the evidence, searched the suspect's home, etc you are now intend to interview the suspect about additional or more serious offences, which may involve a notional arrest, otherwise you may be seen as ambushing the suspect.

CODE C 6

▶ **Legal advice?** – Is the person being legally represented in interview, or received legal advice by telephone? This knowledge is vital in preparing for your interview.

CODE C 11.13 Note 11D

▶ **Unsolicited Comments?** – Has the person made any unsolicited comments? This is common during searches of the person or premises. You will need to ensure that such comments have been properly recorded, in which case they may need to be introduced as an exhibit *(see [C] Exhibits)*. If they have not been properly recorded you will need to do so, possibly on tape in the interview. Be aware that a defence solicitor will invariably have asked their client what statements, if any, they have made and be prepared to challenge any breach of the Codes.

CODE C 11.1A 11.1 11.3

▶ **Prior interviews?** – Has the suspect been informally interviewed? Other officers, possibly more impetuous and less professional than you, may have 'interviewed' the suspect in the course of searching them, or their premises; without the benefit of a caution or legal advice. You must consider repairing the damage by making an opening statement in your interview to the effect that this is the first interview and that neither you nor the suspect should take cognisance of anything done or said before.

Some will argue that the best course of action is to ignore what happened. But the defence solicitor will doubtless be aware of any pre-interview chat and argue at court that any admissions were made under the duress or inducements of others, raising the possibility that your interview will be viewed as 'the fruit of the poisoned tree', and be excluded.

Will it be necessary to put to the suspect any:

| CODE C 11.2A | ❱ **significant statement** – (ie a direct admission of guilt)?
 ❱ **silence** – (ie a failure or refusal to answer questions, or answer them satisfactorily? |

and/or

| CODE C 10.5 A&B | ❱ **special warnings** – give the suspect any special warnings? |

Given the nature of drug offences, there is a high probability of finding objects or substances, such as drugs and paraphernalia, or a likelihood of being found 'at a place or time' when the offence was committed. Good examples would include 'body guards' or 'drivers' found with a drugs dealer at the moment a deal goes down, or those found inside an illicit laboratory.

Comment

The time to introduce any significant statement or silence which occurred before the suspect's arrival at the police station, is dictated by the Codes of Practice and must be put to the suspect at the beginning of the interview.

In contrast, the special warnings under ss36 and 37 of the Criminal Justice and Public Order Act 1994, relate to 'refusals or unsatisfactory answers' to questions put to the suspect in interview. The timing of introducing such special warnings requires careful planning. The process concerning the requirements of the Codes of Practice, namely the five specific points which must be put to the suspect before delivering the special warnings also need to be planned carefully.

There are also special provisions under the Codes for interviews in relation to Drug Trafficking *(see [E] page 184).*

[B] Points to prove

The Misuse of Drugs Act 1971 details all the elements necessary
to prove the key drugs related offences and includes a series of
comprehensive defences. Investigators contemplating a drugs
offence interview must, as part of any necessary preparation,
familiarise themselves with the relevant drugs offences and
defences. This section aims to short cut this process by listing all
the main drugs offences contained within the legislation together
with their points to prove and defences. These offences include:

[1]   Unlawful possession, s5(2)
       (see also [7] Statutory Defences)
       – plus particular defences (s5(4))

[2]   Unlawful supply, s4(3)
       (see also [7] Statutory Defences)

[3]   Possession with intent to supply, s5(3)
       (see also [7] Statutory Defences)

[4]   Unlawful production, s4(2)
       (see also [7] Statutory Defences)

[5]   Cultivation of cannabis, s6(2)
       (see also [7] Statutory Defences)

[6]   Controlled drugs on premises, s8
       [NB statutory defences do not apply]

                              and

[7]   Statutory defences, s28
       (Applicable to [1] - [5] above).

Note:

There are also specific offences prohibiting certain activities in
relation to opium smoking and obstructing an officer searching
premises under a search warrant, or concealing any books, documents or drugs from an inspection of a business lawfully supplying or producing controlled drugs.

[1] UNLAWFUL POSSESSION

(s5(2) Misuse of Drugs Act 1971)

This section makes it an offence for any person to

> 'unlawfully have a controlled drug in their possession'.

This apparently simple definition incorporates a number of key points to prove and includes a series of specific defences, as well as the statutory defences dealt with later *(see [7] Statutory Defences page 175)*. We will start with the points to prove.

[1.i] Points to Prove

'Unlawfully'

Exempting those who may lawful-ly possess such drugs, including:

❱ those who have been prescribed the drug by a doctor
❱ those who possess the drug in the course of their duties, such as police officers; customs and excise officers; authorised couriers or postal workers; forensic scientists and the like
❱ persons acting in the capacity of a doctor, dentist, veterinary practitioner or surgeon, a pharmacist or retail pharmacist
❱ those licensed to possess the drug.

'Possess'

This term includes anything subject to control by the person concerned, even if it is in the custody of another.

Example

> If Page had given some of his drugs to his neighbour Parsons for safe keeping, Page would still possess them. Parsons too would possess the drugs, if he knew that it was a controlled drug he was looking after *(see also [3] Possession with Intent to Supply page 167)*.

It is also possible to jointly possess a controlled drug, if they have joint control. Once again an example may help clarify things:

Example

If Page and Parsons had shared a bed-sit and shared a communal jar of Cannabis, each dipping into it and sharing its contents, both would unlawfully possess it.

Note: Unlawful possession of a controlled drug

R v Searle, and Others ([1971] Crim LR 592 CA), emphasised that mere knowledge of the existence of the controlled drug was not sufficient to amount to 'possession', there must be an element of control. In this instance the fact that various drugs were found in the vehicle being used by the defendants while on holiday did not itself constitute joint possession.

It is also possible to possess something internally, or which exists only by way of 'traces'.

Example

If, on hearing the police entering the building, Page 'necked' the drugs, (ie swallowed them), thereby allowing his body to transform them and radically change their character. Subsequent forensic tests of Page's blood or urine, or evidence of 'traces' of the substance in the container from which he had swallowed should be sufficient proof of unlawful possession.

Comment

Remember that the time and location of the charge for possession may be some point prior to the time and place of arrest and this will probably be determined by interview.

Note – Admission of possession

Bird v Adams ([1972] Crim LR 174 DC), suggests that an admission alone may be sufficient to prove unlawful possession. However, this case was unusual in that the admission revealed in depth knowledge and experience by the suspect.

Despite such decided cases which emphasise that 'unlawful possession' does not depend on proving a sufficient quantity to be usable, the weight of the substance remains relevant, both in terms of the fact of the drug's existence and knowledge of possession. Its weight may suggest the degree to which it was visible, measurable and tangible. The interviewer should attempt to get the suspect to confirm what they believed the substance to be and give its estimated quantity and street value *(see [7] Statutory Defences page 175)*.

[1.ii] Defences

In addition to the Statutory defences *(see [7] page 175)* applicable to this offence there are two 'specific' defences, namely:

[a]   A person knowing or believing it to be a controlled drug took possession of it to prevent another from committing or continuing to commit the offence and as soon as practicable was going to destroy it or give the drug to someone who could lawfully possess it, ie a police officer.

Example

> Page's uncle Bryan finds the drug and decides to throw it in the fire, or deliver it to the police, in order to stop his nephew continuing to possess it unlawfully.

[b]   The person knowing or believing it to be a controlled drug took possession of it, intending to give it to someone who could lawfully possess it, ie a police officer, etc, and as soon as practicable took all reasonable steps to deliver it to such a person.

Example

> Page's neighbour Everett finds some drugs in the communal area of their house and is on his way out of the front door to deliver them to the police, when he is arrested. He would have a defence.

Note

Remember these defences apply only to unlawful possession and do not apply to other offences.

[2] UNLAWFUL SUPPLY

(s4(3), Misuse of Drugs Act 1971)

This section makes it an offence to

'unlawfully supply a controlled drug to another; be concerned in so supplying it; or offer to supply it; or be concerned in making an offer to supply it'.

Once again we shall 'de-construct' the offence and examine each of its component parts.

'Unlawfully'

That is, supply, otherwise than under the various legislation and regulations, eg by means of prescription, or via hospitals, doctors or veterinarians, etc.

'Supply a controlled drug to another'

Supplying includes distributing. If a person bought drugs on behalf of themselves or for friends and handed them out, providing that this was done for the benefit of those who received them. This would be considered supplying, because the person is clearly distributing the drugs. A decided case may help. In *R v Harris* ([1968] 2 All ER 49) a woman injected a man with his own drug claiming that she was assisting him to administer it rather than supply it. She was acquitted of supplying, though arguably she could have been convicted of simple possession.

Note: attempt to supply

By virtue of *Houghton and Smith* ([1975] 3 All ER 1109) and *Mieras v Rees* [1975] Crim LR 224) it must be proved that the substance supplied is a controlled drug (mere belief is not sufficient), though obviously an attempt to commit the offence could be considered *(see 'offer to supply' overleaf)*.

'To be concerned in the supplying of such a drug to another'

This involves some degree of identifiable participation and includes acts such as driving the supplier to or from the place where the actual supply took place, or by protecting him from attack. Similarly 'arranging such transactions' in which controlled drugs are unlawfully supplied would amount to 'be concerned in' *(see also 'offer to supply below).*

'To offer to supply a controlled drug'

In contrast to 'supplying' above, this element of the offence does not require proof that the substance is a controlled drug. Such was the decided case of *Haggard v Mason* (All ER 337), in which a person thought he had acquired LSD – a controlled drug – when in fact he had acquired a substitute, not controlled under the Act.

He then went on to offer the substance to a prospective customer, still believing it to be LSD, thereby committing the offence of 'offering to supply'.

'Offering to supply' also covers instances where the supplier knew that the substance was not a controlled drug, ie *R v Shower* ([1995] Crim LR 400), in which a dealer offered an undercover officer a cream coloured substance, as 'crack cocaine', knowing that in fact it was a 'peanut'. He was convicted of 'offering to supply' on the basis that the offer was sufficient to prove the offence.

Quite simply the offence is complete when the offer is made, rather than when any subsequent transaction was completed.

Example

> If, having planned to steal the doctor's bag containing drugs, etc, Page offered them for sale, in advance, promising his friend 'Dobbo', a desperate drug addict, that he would deliver them in a couple of days, Page would be guilty of this offence *(see also [7] Statutory defences)*.

[3] POSSESSION WITH INTENT TO SUPPLY

(s5(3) Misuse of Drugs Act 1971)

It is an offence for a person to:

> 'have a controlled drug in his possession (whether lawfully or not) with intent to supply it unlawfully to another'.

As usual we will 'de-construct' the offence and examine the 'points to prove' in detail.

'To have a controlled drug in his possession'

This includes the various elements of 'unlawful possession' *(s5(2) see page 162)*.

'Whether lawfully or not'

That is to say persons who are lawfully in possession but nevertheless intend to supply it unlawfully to another. An example of this aspect of the offence will be:

Example

> Tipple, a doctor, can legally possess heroin, but when he gives it to his girlfriend, who is a heroin addict, so that she will remain with him, he commits this offence.

'With intent to supply it unlawfully to another'

Again, decided cases may help with this element of the offence:

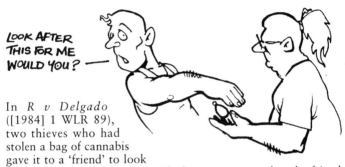

LOOK AFTER
THIS FOR ME
WOULD YOU?

In *R v Delgado*
([1984] 1 WLR 89),
two thieves who had
stolen a bag of cannabis
gave it to a 'friend' to look
after for a couple of hours, with the arrangement that the friend
would return it to them at a specific time and place. Delgado (the
friend) argued he was not supplying the drugs, merely returning
them. It was held that supply within s5(3) meant the transfer of
physical control and the question of ownership or possession was
irrelevant. He was convicted of possession with intent to supply.

In *R v Maginnis* ([1987] 2-All ER 907), the defendant
claimed a package of cannabis found in his car had
been left by a friend who would no doubt have col-
lected it in due course. The decision in this case rein-
forced the earlier one; 'safekeeping' amounted to an
intent to supply; adding that it must be for purpose of
the other person, ie allowing them to use it.

Comment

In the unscrupulous world of the drug dealer there are those who
knowingly possess substances which are not controlled drugs, but
intend to offer them for sale as controlled drugs. This would not
constitute an offence under this section. Though you may consider other offences such as unlawful supply (s4(3)).

Obviously, if the dealer himself believed these fake substances
were controlled drugs, then an offence under the Criminal
Attempts Act 1981 would probably apply.

(See also [7] Statutory defences, page 175.)

[4] UNLAWFUL PRODUCTION

s4(2) Misuse of Drugs Act 1971

It is an offence for a person

> 'unlawfully to produce a controlled drug or to be concerned in the production of a controlled drug'.

Once again we will break down the offence into its component points to prove:

'Unlawfully'

This exempts authorised production by such bodies as drug manufacturing companies, research institutes, registered chemists, etc.

'To "produce" a "controlled drug"'

Both terms are defined by the Misuse of Drugs Act 1971:

> ▶ s37 defines produce as 'manufacture, cultivate, and any other method'

> ▶ Schedule 2 lists all the controlled drugs covered by the legislation.
> *(See Chapter 2 which reproduces the full schedule for your information.)*

Note: Cannabis

There is a specific offence of Cultivating Cannabis *(see facing page)*, which was reputedly introduced to cover a legal loophole concerning immature plants. However the Criminal Law Act 1977 amended the definition of 'Cannabis' to include such plants. Therefore cultivation of cannabis at any stage is arguably covered by this offence. We suggest that you check with your force policy or your local CPS to decide upon the most appropriate charge in relation to a particular case of cultivating cannabis.

Note: Magic mushrooms

It is not an offence to grow, or eat, magic mushrooms, though it is an offence to remove them from their natural state and prepare them by drying them, etc, thereby producing the drug psilocin (Class A controlled drug) *(see Chapter 2)*.

Comment

This is a very wide offence covering everything from the commercial to the domestic, from producing LSD tabs in the kitchen to cultivating cannabis in the airing cupboard. It even covers converting one form of a controlled drug into another form of the same drug (ie *R v Russell* (1992 CR App R 351).

'To be concerned in the production of a controlled drug'

This must involve some identifiable participation (*R v Farr* [1982] Crim LR 745). The mere hiring out of a laboratory for the illicit production of a controlled drug was not sufficient evidence of a offence under this section.

(But see [6] Controlled Drugs on Premises page 173.)
(See also [7] Statutory Defences page 175.)

[5] CULTIVATION OF CANNABIS

(s6(2), Misuse of Drugs Act 1971)

Subject to the Regulations under s7 of the Misuse of Drugs Act 1971, (Authorising and Licensing Activities in Relation to Controlled Drugs)

> 'it is unlawful (for a person) to cultivate
> any plant of the genus cannabis'.

The key terms of this section are 'cultivate' and 'cannabis'. We will deal with each in turn.

'Cultivation'

Cultivation is defined as, 'prepare, till, improve, develop, pay attention to and cherish' ie a range of acts designed to promote growth from planting to picking.

Comment

In reality, your problems will be more concerned with identifying the plant than with proving cultivation. The latter will involve observing the quantity, position and health of the plants concerned and questions as to the steps taken to promote growth, such as potting, feeding, watering, etc are essential. You may well find a profusion of cannabis plants being irrigated and grown under glass or artificial lights, sometimes secreted away in lofts, cupboards and the like. *(See also Chapter 2, and [4] Unlawful Production (s4(2) page 169.)*

Note: Hydroponics

Hydroponics is a system of growing plants without soil and involves them being suspended in water or supported in an inert medium such as rockwool or sand. Nutrients are put in to the water supply to feed the plants with the lighting system and temperature being carefully controlled. Growing cannabis plants in this way will require the use of expensive sophisticated equipment and if such systems are discovered it could prove beneficial evidentially to involve a forensic scientist at an early stage of the investigation.

Cannabis

Cannabis is defined as:

> 'Any plant of the genus cannabis, or any part of the plant except
>
> ▶ Cannabis Resin
>
> ▶ Any of the following products which have been separated from the rest of the plant
>
>> – the mature stalk
>> – fibre produced from the mature stalk
>> – seed of any such plant.'

(See also [7] Statutory defences page 175.)

[6] CONTROLLED DRUGS ON PREMISES

(s8, Misuse of Drugs Act 1971)

A person commits an offence if

> **'being the occupier, or concerned in the management, of any premises, he knowingly permits or suffers'** any of the following activities to take place on those premises:

❱ unlawfully producing or attempting to produce a controlled drug
❱ unlawfully supplying or attempting to supply a controlled drug to another or offering to supply a controlled drug unlawfully to another
❱ preparing opium for smoking
❱ smoking cannabis, cannabis resin or prepared opium.

Once again we will explore the various elements of this extensive offence.

'Occupier'

This is an area which might be better understood by reference to a couple of detailed cases:

R v Tao [1976] (All ER 65) extended the term 'occupier' beyond the concepts of ownership and exclusive control to include owner-occupiers by way of a mortgage, those who rent premises and those who have a licence entitling them to exclude from the premises persons who might offend under this section.

In *R v Magford and others* ([1970] Crim LR 401), two sisters who held a party while their parents were away were deemed not to be the occupiers and their degree of control (by inviting guests) did not amount to control under the Act *(but consider 'concerned in the management' overleaf).*

Comment

Such questions relating to 'occupiers' are best resolved with the benefit of research and advice from others with supervisory experience, or specialist legal knowledge.

'Concerned in the management'

This refers not to management of the premises, but management of the activities carried on within the premises (*R v Josephs and Christie* (1977) 65 CR App R253). In fact even those with no legal rights, such as squatters, can commit this offence – for example, those who organise a 'rave' involving the wholesale taking of drugs, providing they run, organise or plan the event.

'Any premises'

'Premises' is not defined in the Act, but probably includes a wide range of premises from castle to cattle shed.

'Knowingly permits or suffers'

Covers a whole spectrum of conduct including:

▶ actual knowledge of what was taking place
▶ wilful blindness by shutting one's eyes to the obvious
▶ recklessness.

In *R v Souter* ([1971] All ER1151) a person who accommodated persons addicted to drugs, prohibited those who he knew were in possession of drugs and displayed notices on the premises to the effect that the police would be called to anyone suspected to be unlawfully 'in possession'. Following a police raid which found a small quantity of drugs and signs of drug usage, he was charged but subsequently acquitted, having been deemed by the court to have taken reasonable steps to prevent misconduct.

[7] STATUTORY DEFENCES

(s28, Misuse of Drugs Act 1971)

This contains three defences which apply
to the following offences under the Act.

- S4(2) Unlawful Production
- S4(3) Unlawful Supply
- S5(2) Unlawful Possession
- S5(3) Possession with Intent to Supply
- S6(2) Unlawful Cultivation of Cannabis
- S9   Offences Related to Opium

The three defences are as follows:

▶ lack of knowledge of fact alleged

▶ lack of knowledge of controlled drug

▶ belief that it was a drug he was entitled to produce,
supply, possess, etc.

In each of the three defences, the prosecution must first establish
a *prima facie* case against the defendant. It is only then that the
accused needs to show on a balance of probabilities that he was
not at fault in accordance with s28.

[7.i] Lack of knowledge of the fact alleged

To use this defence a person must show three things:

> ▶ he did not know the existence of some fact alleged
> ▶ he did not suspect the existence of that fact
> ▶ he had no reason to suspect the existence of that fact.

The 'fact' must be one that it is necessary for the prosecution to prove.

Example

> You approach Page and Pullen who are walking together in the high street. Page is carrying a small piece of cannabis and to avoid being found in possession, slips it into Pullen's pocket without his knowledge. Pullen would have a defence to 'unlawful possession' because he could show that he did not know he was carrying the cannabis, and had no reason to suspect what was going on.

In a case of unlawful possession 'knowledge' is a 'key fact' the prosecution have to prove.

[7.ii] Lack of knowledge of fact that the substance was a Controlled Drug

Where a suspect is found in possession of a controlled drug he may be acquitted if he satisfies the court of three things:

- he did not believe it was a controlled drug
- he did not suspect it was a controlled drug
- he had no reason to suspect it was a controlled drug.

Example

> Hook gives his employee Bell a package to deliver in the normal course of his employment. He tells Bell that it contains tobacco. The package is found to contain cannabis. Bell would have a defence because he did not know, did not suspect and he had no reason to suspect it was a controlled drug.

However when a person found in possession of a controlled drug argues he thought that it was a different controlled drug he has no defence.

Example

Andrews is found in possession of cocaine and states in interview that he thought it was amphetamine – he could not claim this as a defence.

[7.iii] A belief that it was a drug he was entitled to produce, supply or possess

To use this defence the person must show two things:

 ❱ he believed it was a controlled drug or a particular controlled drug *and*

 ❱ he believed that had it been that controlled drug, or a particular controlled drug, he would have committed no offence.

Example

Turnbull, a registered drug addict, goes to a chemist with a prescription for a particular drug, but the chemist makes a mistake and gives him another controlled drug instead. Turnbull is now in unlawful possession of this second drug but he would have a defence because he could show that he believed it to be the drug he was allowed to possess as a registered drug addict.

[C] Exhibits in interview

Introducing exhibits and the timing of their production is an important part of any interview and the way they are referred to is evidentially vital. In drugs cases there are often numerous exhibits that need to be accounted for and require clarification of their purpose. We have mentioned how seemingly innocent articles such as: 'Jiff' lemons, 'spoons' with burnt bowls, 'catalogues' with squares cut from their pages, 'silver paper', rolls of 'cling film', and 'rizla' cigarette paper packets may all require an explanation from a suspect, (in addition to any drugs recovered).

The drugs themselves may need to be packaged or re-packaged in interview, *(see Chapter 6)*, and this procedure can be very time consuming. However it is vital that they are clearly identified using their police 'Item number', and properly connected to the matter under investigation, clearly stating how and where they were recovered for the benefit of the tape.

The timing of introducing exhibits to the suspect during interview can enhance its quality, and planning for this is crucial. Consider introducing the exhibits at the beginning of an interview to get it over with, allowing you to concentrate on the interview proper.

Be clear when you describe items and remember the tape machine doesn't have eyes.

Example

When interviewing Page, PC Robin Cross wishes to introduce the small wrap of Amphetamine which is police item number RC3. It would be acceptable for PC Cross to introduce it by saying, 'For the benefit of the tape I am now showing Mr Page a red-coloured paper wrap, containing a quantity of cream-coloured powder. This is police item-number RC 3. You could then go on to question Page about its identity, value, weight, the circumstances of it being found and where he got it from.

By getting into the habit of introducing your exhibits in a particular way you will appear more professional in the eyes of others.

Comment

Be careful not to allow suspects to handle exhibits in interview. Some drug suspects will attempt to swallow (neck) substances, or blow away powders in the interview room, given the opportunity. Others will deliberately touch objects to compromise any fingerprint evidence on such things as cling film wraps.

[D] Conducting the interview

Interviewing drugs suspects is not always straight forward and there are many possible permutations of offences to be considered *(see [B] Points to Prove page 161)*. What may appear at first as a simple possession could amount to possession with intent to supply, whereas larger amounts of a drug may actually be for personal use. Although the circumstances of the seizure and subsequent arrest may point to particular offences, the interview is vital in determining what, if any, is the correct charge.

[1] STARTING THE INTERVIEW

Q. How do I start the interview?
A. By now you have fully prepared your agenda and amassed a folder of relevant material to assist you in the interview (and brought your copy of the Codes of Practice to the interview in case it is needed):

▶ You will be collating the relevant 'points to prove' and 'defences' for all the possible offences; collecting relevant statements, (possibly accompanied by a summary to give you a chronological sequence of events, together with a note of any ambiguities or inconsistencies you want to nail down); making a summary of the suspects basic details, associates and offending history; and considering any tricky PACE issues you may have to confront.

▶ You have also prepared a box of exhibits, all properly labelled, and a schedule of how and when you plan to use them in interview.

▶ Finally you have prepared the room, yourself and your mind, reading up all the relevant information and being open and flexible in your thinking. Most important of all you have your purpose, objectives and a plan of how you are going to carry out the interview.

▶ Some experienced officers also prepare an opening statement which sets out the facts and your initial agenda. A typical one would go something like: *'Good morning, my name is [..........]*
[Now having gone through the necessary legal preliminaries at the beginning of the interview it is time to start the interview proper.]

'You were arrested at [place-date and time] for the offence of [..........]. At the time of your arrest a brown resinous substance was recovered from the breast pocket of your shirt. This substance is police item number RC2, and the purpose of this interview is to investigate the matter. So the first thing I need to know is your explanation of the events surrounding your arrest. Tell me what happened?'

[2] INTRODUCING EVIDENCE

Q. What problems can I face in introducing evidence?

A. During the course of the interview you will probably need to introduce evidence from a variety of sources. Here are a few ideas and suggestions to help you do it properly:

[2.i] Exhibits

(See also [C] Exhibits in Interview page178)

Remember an exhibit produced is twice as good as an exhibit described and the effect is often enhanced – with your agenda better controlled – by keeping them hidden in a folder or a box until the moment you want to introduce them. Once dealt with they are best out of the way and not left about to distract the interviewee. Remember to quote the exhibit number. It is essential to prove continuity and prevent confusion each time you produce a new exhibit.

[2.ii] Forensic evidence

It is imperative that, having read a report from the Forensic Science Service, you understand it fully. You might even consider taking advice from the help desk if you are unclear about its findings or scientific terms. Remember you have to explain to the suspect in clear, simple language what the forensic scientist has said. Once again some experienced investigators preface the introduction of a report with a little prepared statement about the accuracy and relevance of such forensic evidence. But be careful when introducing or describing such evidence, not to 'gild the lily' or you may find your interview being excluded.

[2.iii] Informant information

An informant should never be compromised in interview. If when reviewing the information prior to interview you fear that questioning may lead the suspect to the identity of the informant you must liaise with the informant's handler or controller, even if they are outside your force, and to seek guidance from a supervisory officer; bearing in mind the possible consequences to the informant if their identity is revealed.

[2.iv] Surveillance evidence

Increased pro-active policing, especially in relation to drugs, means that you may get the benefit of such evidence, but it remains a very sensitive area and interviewers should not reveal:

> ❱ static observation points
> ❱ types, makes, models, numbers or descriptions of vehicles or the names or descriptions of operatives
> ❱ anything which discloses the method of surveillance used, especially that involving 'technical' surveillance equipment.

You may find the surveillance report difficult and contradictory, if so seek advice from those who compiled them. You may find it helpful to construct your own chronological sequence using some form of time graph for quick reference, allowing instant comparison between what the interviewee says and what you know. Remember that if you do produce a time graph it will be 'unused material' declared to the Crown Prosecution Service.

[3] MAKING SENSE OF THE INTERVIEWEE'S REPLIES

Q. What do I do if the interviewee uses street terms which I do not understand?

Example

I ask Page to explain his possession and he says something like: 'The wrap's a G of whizz. I've just scored it from the pub. You've got my works, which I was going to use to fix it.

A. The answer is to familiarise yourself with the terms used by drug users, as this will help you to relate to your interviewee. However, you must remember to get your interviewee to translate the street language into 'evidential English' for the benefit of others. You may need to help in that process and once again an understanding of the jargon can be of great assistance when framing the right question. Page's statement would translate as:

'The paper fold in my possession contains a gram of amphetamine which I have just bought from someone in the pub. You have recovered my needle and syringe which I was going to use to inject the drug.'

To help you we have included an appendix to this chapter, listing a number of commonly used drugs 'expressions'.

[E] Drug trafficking

The various drugs trafficking legislation allows the prosecution to apply to the courts to make an order where drugs traffickers have been convicted and they have gained benefit from drug offences.

The principal Acts relating to the sequestration of assets and investigation of the finances of criminals in relation to drug trafficking are:

- ❯ The Misuse of Drugs Act 1971
- ❯ The Drugs Trafficking Act 1994.

CODE C 11.4	Questioning in relation to confiscation of assets, is normally conducted in a separate interview after completing a formal interview.

This section aims to give you an overview of this legislation, as well as mentioning the specific things that you the investigator can and must do to assist the court to seize the assets from those who profit from the illegal drugs trade.

We will deal with each of the key relevant Acts in turn:

[1] THE MISUSE OF DRUGS ACT 1971 (S27)

This Act deals with anything which relates to the offence and is capable of being forfeited and/or destroyed. If a motor car has been used in the commission of the offence, not only does it become an exhibit but it can be forfeited. (However, account should be taken of the age, condition and relative value of the car, and before any vehicle is taken into police possession, we suggest you consult your force policy and check with a supervisory officer.)

[2] THE DRUGS TRAFFICKING ACT 1994

'Drug trafficking' is defined in s1 (Drug Trafficking Act 1994) and a 'drug trafficking offence is defined in the same section as:

> 'Production, supply and possession for supply of controlled drugs within the UK. Assisting in, or inducing the commission of a drugs offence (committed outside the UK) which is punishable under corresponding law.'

These offences are:

▶ Improper Importation (s50(2) or (3) of the Customs and Excise Management Act 1979)

▶ Exportation (s68(2))

▶ Fraudulent Evasion (s170) in connection with a prohibition or restriction on importation or exportation, having effect by virtue of s3 of the Misuse of Drugs Act 1971;

▶ An offence under s12 Criminal Justice (International Co-operation) Act 1990 (manufacture or supply of substance specified in Sched 2 to that Act)

▶ An offence under s19 of that Act (using ship for illicit traffic in controlled drugs)

▶ An offence under s49, 50 or 51 of this Act or s14 of the Criminal Justice (International Co-operation) Act 1990 (which makes, in relation to Scotland and Northern Ireland, provision corresponding to s49 of this Act);

▶ Conspiracy to commit any of the offences shown above

▶ Attempting to commit any of these offences

▶ Inciting another person to commit any of these offences, whether under s19 of the Misuse of Drugs Act 1971 or at common law; and includes aiding, abetting, counselling or procuring the commission of any of the above offences.

S
This Act also applies to Scotland and in Northern Ireland.

When a person is convicted of a drug trafficking offence, the Crown Court can order the confiscation of their assets if it can be shown that they have benefited from drugs trading.

Comment

In routine day-to-day policing, you are unlikely to deal with such exotic offences with the exception of Production, Supply and Possession for Supply of Controlled Drugs, or Attempts to commit these offences.

The '**gaining benefit**' can be shown in a number of ways. If investigation shows that a person has assets which cannot be shown to come from a legitimate source – such as purchased through legitimate earnings, or inherited – then the court can assume that those assets have come from drug trafficking. In the case of drug trafficking offences the burden of proof required to show benefit and assets is the test applied to civil proceedings, that of 'on the balance of probabilities' rather than that of 'beyond reasonable doubt'. Consequently drug traffickers are often keen to talk to the police to explain their assets.

Money and drugs in the possession of the drugs dealer can also be used to assess benefit.

It is important for the investigating officer to obtain as much detail as possible about the finances, assets etc of such drug dealers. Information, surveillance, past history etc can all help to build up a picture of their financial situation which will be of great benefit to those specialists tasked with investigating drug trafficking offences. It is they who will, in all probability, gain access to their financial records, enquire into their business and interview them about these matters.

Having given you an overview of the Drug Trafficking legislation, it seems relevant to ask the question: 'What do I need to do?'

The answer is simple, you can play a major part in the success of this process by ensuring that during searches of premises, you look for evidence that may provide information of a person's financial affairs.

Often those involved in drug trafficking show signs of conspicuous consumption well beyond their means, though this is not always the case.

In one instance we know, a ship's steward led a double life which came to light only through finding a building society paying-in slip. He appeared to be an average family man with a second hand car, a semi' and a dog. Inquiries discovered a luxury flat, a mistress and a brand new cabriolet.

When an arrest is made and premises searched, evidence of income and expenditure should be seized. Pay slips, details of benefit claims, hire purchase agreements, invoices, bank and building society accounts, investments and incomes are among the documents which should be seized or copied.

Evidence of unlawful income can be useful in the criminal case, over and above assessing benefit after a trial, and can be used to strengthen a case.

All in all much depends on your powers of observation and your judgement.

Note

Finally check with your own force instructions as it may be prudent to serve a section 19 Drug Trafficking Act 1996. Notice to enable the court to recover assets in the event 'the trafficker' absconds.

[F] Appendix: glossary of terms used on the drug scene

Acid	LSD or other hallucinogens
Acid Head	LSD user
Angel Dust	Phencyclidine
Barbs	Barbiturates
Bennies	Benzedrine
Bhang	Cannabis
Biscuits	Ecstasy
Blow	To smoke Cannabis
Busted	Arrested
Buy	Make a purchase of drugs
Buzz	Moderate euphoric reaction to drugs
C	Cocaine
CAPS	Capsule of drugs
Charged Up	Under the influence of drugs
Cold Turkey	Symptoms as a result of sudden withdrawal of drugs
Coke	Cocaine
Crank Up	To inject drugs
Cut	To adulterate drugs with another substance
Dealer	Supplier of drugs
Dennis the Menace	Ecstasy
Dexies	Dexedrine
Dope	Cannabis
Downers	Sedatives
Eighth	One eighth of an ounce
'E'	Ecstasy

Factory	Place where illicit drugs are manufactured
Fix	To inject drugs
Fixed up	Under the influence of drugs
Floating	Under the influence of drugs
Fuzz	The police
Gear	Drugs in general
'G'	Gram
Ganja¡	Cannabis
Grass	Herbal Cannabis
'H'	Heroin
Hang up	Withdrawal process
Hash	Cannabis (usually herbal)
Hit	An injection of a drug
Hooked¡	Addicted
Horse	Heroin
Jellies or Jelly Babies	Temazepam
Joint	On roll of Cannabis (Cannabis cigarette)
Juice	Anabolic Steroids
Junk	Narcotics
Junkie	Addict
Kick the Habit	Get off the drugs
A Kilo	2.2 pounds - weight
Marijuana	Cannabis
Mainliner	One who injects directly into the vein
Micro Dots	LSD

Necking	Disposing of the drug by swallowing it
OD	Overdose drugs death
Peddler	Supplier
Pep Pills	Amphetamine
Pick Up	Make a purchase of drugs
Plant	Drugs planted on a person without his knowledge
Pot	Cannabis
Pusher	Drug supplier
Reefer	Cannabis cigarette
Roaches	Butts of Cannabis cigarettes
Roids	Anabolic Steroids
Rugby Balls	Temazepam
Scag	Heroin
Score	Make a purchase
Script	A prescription (NHS)
Shit	Cannabis
Shoot Up	To inject drugs
Skin Popping	To inject drugs under the skin
Smack	Heroin
Snort	Inhale drugs up the nose
Snow	Cocaine
Speed	Amphetamine
Speedball	Heroin and Cocaine mixture
Stash	Hidden supply of drugs
Stick	Cannabis in shape of stick
Stoned	Under the influence of drugs

Stuff	General term for drugs
Uppers	Stimulants
Weed	Cannabis bush
Weight	1 kilo of drugs
Whizz	Amphetamine
Wobbly Eggs	Temazepam
Works	Needle and syringe
Wrap	Drugs wrapped up

Please add your own known terms to this list.

Author's note

Street expressions change with the fashion and are constantly being added to, and vary from region to region. This glossary does not claim to include all the drug related jargon, but rather provides a basis for your own local and relevant expressions.

Index